D1153991

THE GIRLS

A biography of Frances Loring and Florence Wyle

the girls

by Rebecca Sisler

CLARKE, IRWIN & COMPANY LIMITED

Toronto   Vancouver

© 1972 by Clarke, Irwin & Company Limited

ISBN 0-7720-0578-8

Printed in Canada

To Edith MacIver

ACKNOWLEDGEMENTS

For their generosity in contributing recollections and impressions of Loring and Wyle, I am deeply indebted to at least fifty of their former friends and associates.

Thanks are also due to the National Gallery of Canada, The Art Gallery of Ontario and the London Public Library and Art Museum, for their co-operation in opening records and archival material for my use.

I also wish to record my gratitude to Christopher Chapman for allowing free access to the research material taped in preparation for his film on Loring and Wyle.

R.S.

The excerpts in chapter seven are reprinted from *Poems*, by Florence Wyle, The Ryerson Press, by permission of McGraw-Hill Ryerson Limited.

This project was completed with the assistance of a Canada Council grant under its Canadian Horizons Program.

PHOTO CREDITS

Portrait of Wyle by Loring. Photo by Herb Nott, Toronto.

Portrait of Loring by Wyle. Photo by Herb Nott, Toronto.

The Wembley selection committee. Photo by H. Hands, Ottawa.

Portrait of Frederick Varley by Wyle. Photo by Jean Gainfort Merrill, Toronto.

Portrait of A. Y. Jackson by Wyle. Photo by Jean Gainfort Merrill, Toronto.

Study of a Girl by Wyle. Photo by The Smiths, Toronto.

War Memorial, St. Stephen, N.B. Photo by Pringle and Booth, Toronto.

The Church before 1952. Photo by Herb Nott, Toronto.

The Church, 1958. Photo, Information Canada Photothèque.

The Girls having tea. Photo by Gilbert A. Milne, Toronto.

The Girls at work, 1952. Photo by Gilbert A. Milne, Toronto.

Clay Models of *Sir Robert Borden*. Photo by Horst Ericht.

Frances Loring with portrait of Sir Frederick Banting. Photo by Everett Roseborough, Toronto.

Interior of studio, 1958. Photo, Information Canada Photothèque.

Florence Wyle at work in her studio. Photo by Eric Christensen for *The Globe and Mail*.

Florence Wyle with *Young Mother*. Photo by Ashley & Crippen Ltd., Toronto.

The author and publishers are also grateful to the Loring-Wyle Estate for making available pictures from the collections of Miss Loring and Miss Wyle.

THE GIRLS

PROLOGUE

Bohemians? Hippies? Both terms have been used in an attempt to describe their appearance. Certainly anyone who remembers catching sight of the two women shopping near the corner of Yonge and St. Clair in Toronto will recognize the aptness of the analogy.

They would be proceeding along the street, oblivious of the impression they were creating, the one large majestic figure cruising along with the dignity of a ship under full sail, the other tiny figure following in her wake—bristly, bemused, cursing away under her breath about the noise and fumes from the wretched automobiles. Both would be wearing trousers, men's shoes, baggy coats with scarves dangling from the neckline, and moth-eaten berets pulled down over one ear.

Some passers-by would stare in obvious disapproval of the outlandish get-ups. Some would titter at the incongruity of the pair. Others, more perceptive, might think that these odd-looking women would be interesting to know. Those who *did* know them, realized that they were neither Bohemian nor hippie. Eccentric perhaps. Original certainly. They had their own unique and unconventional life style. But then, as one acquaintance pointed out, they were no more peculiar than other artists.

For artists they were. The Girls, as they were generally known, were, in fact, sculptors.

Their old church studio at 110 Glenrose Avenue was somewhat off-beat for the genteel community that Moore Park had become. Newcomers to the neighbourhood raised eyebrows and averted glances from the paint peeling from the building and the shrubbery growing rather too luxuriantly. But those who could see past the scruffy paint and the tangled shrubbery knew that here was the hub of all that was vital and exciting in the Toronto art world of the twenties and thirties. For nearly fifty years, the studio in that old church was one of the most fascinating gathering places in the country.

"Do sit down!" Frances would warmly urge a visitor—a young artist, perhaps, dropping in for a chat in the late afternoon.

Sit down? Where? The place is full to overflowing with every conceivable object. Chairs are piled with newspapers, books, photographs, boxes. Things are put in "convenient" places—convenient, that is, for old people with arthritis who can't bend down or reach up to out-of-the-way shelves. "Cluttered?" the Girls say, puzzled, if an undiscerning visitor expresses dismay or disapproval. "But we have things where they are handy! All sculptors have studios full of work which they can't afford to put into permanent materials." Best not to press that too far.

Sherry for the visitor is, after a lengthy search, unearthed from beneath a modelling stand; a box of biscuits, from the casting room.

"If you have to smoke, better go downstairs. Miss Wyle is allergic to cigarette smoke," Frances cautions protectively.

"Oh, sit over there by the fireplace and the smoke will go up the flue," Florence intervenes.

Finally, an ancient chair is cleared of its collection of objects, and the visitor, having unobtrusively brushed away a little stone dust, sits down. He looks cautiously around him at the work of the two sculptors, crowding around the sitting area in front of the fireplace.

A heroic plaster hockey player, towering above the other pieces, guards forever an imaginary goal. A bust of Sir Frederick Banting presides with dignity over the circle. A bronze baby peers into the sherry from the arms of a lyric, sculpted mother. A graceful carving in Carrara marble stands to one side on the workstand under the skylight. In the fading afternoon light, the backward arc of a female figure seems to fall like a slow flow of water, and the visitor learns without surprise that it is called "Sea and Shore."

Florence snatches up her hammer and a toothed chisel and taps lightly at a spot beside the navel.

"I keep telling her to leave well enough alone. Not to overdo it." Frances sighs.

4

"I'll stop when it's done," Florence asserts. "Just noticed the light didn't hit true on that spot. There, better now, isn't it? How is your own work going?"

"Yes, do tell us about it!" Frances, tied to the couch with yet another bout of arthritis racking her knees, is hungry for news. "Any word of that commission yet? No? Those architects are so obtuse! They all go around moaning, 'Oh, we've not got a Michelangelo. Oh, if only we had a Michelangelo!' Well, what would they do with him if they had him? They'd let him starve. They wouldn't give him a chance."

"Idiots!" Nothing annoys Florence like artistic apathy and indecision. "Don't know good sculpture from trash. But keep going. Our good sculptors have got to keep going! Of course, you younger people don't know enough about anatomy. You don't know. . . ."

After a time the young artist rises, makes his way around the crowding sculptures, and leaves the studio, grateful for the visit, reconvinced in his purpose. The work is worth the doing. For him, as for so many artists through so many years, the Church has once more been a place of confirmation.

The Girls came to the church on Glenrose Avenue in 1920. They had shared a studio over a carpenter's shop at the corner of Church and Lombard streets. For seven years they had worked away together, interested only in the great physical space of their studio, indifferent to the squalid physical area outside, amused, probably, by the concern of the local police who considered the district unsafe and unsuitable for two attractive young women. "Keep a special eye out for those girls!" the Chief would caution Charles Taylor who walked that beat at night.

Although the Girls could rise above the seamier doings of the area, they could not ignore a notice to vacate when the building came under new management. What to do and where to go? They were in full professional swing and could not stop the rhythm of their production. They needed space for their work; they needed time to complete their commissions. Then came word of an old abandoned Anglican church up in the woods north of Toronto.

The first Christ Church Deer Park had stood for years on the

5

corner of Yonge Street and Lawton Boulevard. The white frame building, contained on its pie-shaped wedge of land by a white picket fence, was a distinctive landmark. But by 1910 the parish's growing congregation called for a larger structure. The original board-and-batten church bowed out in favour of a solid, respectable, red brick building.

The schoolhouse, which had been part of the original church property and which had complemented the frame church architecturally, was moved over to orchard land on Glenrose Avenue. For several years it served as a gospel hall, bringing some comfort perhaps to the dozen or so houses that huddled behind the trees on the unpaved road. Whatever comfort the hall provided was not long lasting, for the mission failed. The weathered red-frame building, roofed with flapping tar-paper and plunked down on cedar piles, was put up for sale, but there was no great rush of buyers. Not even at $3200. Then word of it reached the Girls.

They walked up from Walker Avenue, which was the end of the car line, and over the rustic bridge which spanned the Vale of Avoca at St. Clair, and along Glenrose Avenue to the forlorn and empty building which was the Church.

"What a magnificent studio!"

"But it's so far out," a friend warned. "Architects and patrons will never get out there to see you!"

The warning came too late and went unheeded; having once seen the lofty ceiling of the Church—as it was now referred to by local residents—the Girls were already picturing themselves working away in all that space. Besides, they had been committed for some time now to their lifelong mania for collecting derelicts. How could they resist the appeal of a derelict church?

"We really should come and cheer it up," Florence concluded. There was nothing for it but to borrow money and make the down payment.

Their moving-in was observed with intense curiosity.

First the truck pulled up and began unloading the sculptures—"religious statues!" Children raced away into their houses calling, "Mother! There's a new church moving in across the road!" Lace curtains were pulled discreetly aside. Then the Girls themselves

6

arrived. Lace curtains twitched; hidden viewers stared, blinked, and stared again. Women wearing trousers!

The settling-in was no less interesting for the neighbours. As the Girls began to fix up the Church, there was a sudden surge of outdoor activity up and down the street. Trouser-clad women chopping wood and rolling stones? Out came the brooms to sweep the porches. Women climbing ladders and hammering nails? Out came the shears to prune the shrubs. The Girls were so intent on getting the Church ready to live in and work in that they neither saw the stares nor questioned the intensity of outdoor activity.

When asked in later life about the local reaction at their moving into the Church, they said there had been no particular problems. People had been friendly and neighbourly. There had only been one uncomfortable episode. A friend had decided to give them a house-warming party, which had somehow exceeded its modest intentions and developed into an extravagant costume party. The night was hot, the large doorway was open, and the comings and goings of the oddly dressed-up folk pushed neighbourhood curiosity beyond controllable limits. The sight of a woman lounging in front of the open doorway in a rather transparent pyjama garment attracted a steady parade of passers-by.

"I think it speaks well of us," Frances observed, "that we've managed to outlive that."

To put it mildly, the first years were difficult. Life was primitive Water came from a neighbour's pump. Plumbing was of the outdoor variety. It took the vital endurance and careless courage of youth to survive a winter in that drafty shell of a building.

The first winter was spent, of dire necessity, in close proximity to the great pot-bellied beast of a stove. When stoked up, its great round belly would send off a tremendous blast of heat, which, unfortunately, obeying the laws of conduction, rose immediately into the vaulted heights of the large room. Frances and Florence worked within range of the stove's heat and slept, rolled in blankets, as close as possible to the friendly fire. (But the fire would go out, and water placed under the stove for the dogs and cats would be frozen by morning.)

And, naturally, they bathed in its heat. One cold day Frances had

7

her bathtub pulled up beside the expansive heat of the stove, when the door opened, and two prospective worshippers entered. The men fled in horror, leaving the dripping sculptor chuckling and feeling, "quite like Susanna with the Elders."

As the Girls sagely remarked, "It's well to be young if you're going to be a sculptor. Until you get adjusted at any rate."

The following year they did manage to settle in rather more comfortably. With a contribution which they received from Frances' father, they had the breezy spaces down below blocked off and a partial basement excavated. The awkward front entrance porch was dragged around to the back and used as a chicken house. Under Florence's tender care, a small flock of chickens, named after members of the Group of Seven, provided them with eggs—to the tune of much cackling. Answering complaints that the chickens made too much noise, the Girls claimed that this was due to the fact that they were named after the Group; whenever they laid an egg they had to make a great to-do about it to be sure everyone noticed.

By the second winter they were comfortably installed—at least by their uncritical standards. The Church even had a foundation. By chance, the contractor who was hired to put in their foundation was at the same time engaged in wrecking the second Christ Church Deer Park, which was being torn down to make way for the widening of Yonge Street. He salvaged the brick from the second church and incorporated it into the foundation at 110 Glenrose. Thus it happened that parts of the two discarded church properties were amalgamated.

The Girls also had built a monumental brick fireplace which opened into the dining area in the basement, and into the studio above on the main level, before culminating in a great pyramidal chimney.

Nevertheless, in spite of the noble pot-bellied beast and the great brick fireplace, Florence and Frances were referred to as "The Cheerful Children of the Chilly Church" in a Toronto paper of 1925. And when Sophia Buckingham and Elizabeth Gordon (Mrs. Walter Gordon) arrived for lessons on chill winter mornings in the thirties, they had to break the ice around the rims of the clay tubs before starting to sculpt. Their hands would be like chunks of ice by the time the clay was kneaded into working form. (The painful arthritic knuckles of the Girls' old age were no doubt due to those early difficult times.)

Models, of course, found the studio absolutely frigid. A frozen pose, literally. During the winter months, the naked model posed for brief periods while the clay designs were worked on, and then sat shivering, swathed in blankets.

"Poor lamb!" Frances sympathized with real concern. Florence would be likely to react more practically by throwing another armload of wood into the ravenous belly of the stove.

One model was less willing to cope with such pioneer conditions. The Girls, needing a male model for the figure of Christ, for a sculpture commissioned by the Church of St. Mary Magdalene, brightly and innocently advertised for one in the newspaper. They found themselves confronted with an incredible number and variety of out-of-luck regulars who evidently thought they had the necessary qualifications. One with a suitable face and figure was chosen. After taking a close look at the working conditions, he retreated to the privacy of the bedroom vestry, presumably to undress. Instead, he seized whatever valuables the room contained, and quietly let himself out of the stained-glass window.

Architects and patrons began to find their way to the Church despite the fact that it was so far out of the city. So, too, did artists, musicians, writers, and friends of all shapes and descriptions. The architects did not always come to commission, nor the patrons to buy, but there was enough money to keep the fires burning and something in the pot for guests. Gradually the Church became a natural centre for scores of local people interested in the arts. Visiting writers or artists were almost always brought out to enjoy the hospitality of the Church Girls.

One such visitor repaid their hospitality in the performance of his art. The Church was at that time infested with rats. Both Frances and Florence were very soft-hearted when it came to animals, and neither would have dreamed of setting out traps or poison. The rats flourished and threatened to become a plague.

One evening, Huntley Gordon, a friend who was connected with

9

the publishing business, telephoned to ask if he might come and bring along a small party of friends, including a musician from Scotland. Of course he could come, and his friends too, Scottish and otherwise.

The musician's instrument was the bagpipes, which he had happened to bring with him, just in case. Huntley, a Scotsman himself and no stranger to bagpipes, was anxious to experience their effect in the vaulted reaches of the Church. The piper, in his kilts, piped away until the Church reverberated to the rafters. He piped until his audience was nearly driven out into the street.

Delilah, the studio dog, miserable and in obvious pain, crawled on her stomach over to Florence, buried her head in her mistress' lap, and howled, "Ow oo, oo, oo, oo, oo!"

But the Scotsman continued to pipe. He piped until, unseen and unheard, the last rat abandoned the Church. For years to come, no rat came near.

The parties were not always so dramatic, but they generated great interest and were widely popular. It seems difficult to pinpoint just what made them so good. There was little drinking, for no one had money for much of that. There was no dancing. There was simply a crowd of congenial people enjoying themselves in distinctive surroundings. Certainly the unusual church-like setting and the studio atmosphere contributed to the success of the gatherings. But they were made particularly convivial and lively by the warmth and undemanding friendliness of the Girls. Those who attended the parties still claim they were the best in the whole country.

On a Saturday night it was possible to run into almost anyone at the Church. When a neighbour who used to attend was asked who would be there, she said, "Everybody!"

"Everybody" included A. Y. Jackson and the various members of the Group of Seven, and Barker Fairley, the renowned scholar of German philosophy, and Ashley and Crippen, the photographers. And, of course, Keith MacIver, the prospector, who had made the Girls' dining room table from the old front door of the Crippen house down the street. And also Robert Flaherty, the Arctic photographer, who had just filmed "Nanook of the North." And, usually, Professor Anderson, who taught Philosophy at the University of

Toronto. And Gwendolyn Williams, the well-known piano accompanist. And Adolph Koldofsky, the violinist. And sometimes Madame Jeanne Dusseau, the singer. And, well . . . everybody.

Yvonne McKague Housser attended parties at the Church as a very young painter. She had grown up in a family of conventional background, and for her the gatherings in the studio were exciting. These parties were her first contact with the living world of art, and she found the atmosphere "heady."

Not that they were wild parties. Florence was dead against drinking. Frances, on the other hand, enjoyed nothing more than a convivial drink with friends. As in many things when people of two totally opposed opinions share the same quarters, there had to be a compromise. On this particular issue, it was Florence who gave in. Although she never touched a drop herself, she did not inflict her disapproval on their guests. Besides, her friends were her friends, and it was impossible for them to offend her. Professor Larry Lawson, then a young reporter with the *Star* and sometimes a little indiscreet with alcohol, remembers her literally going the second mile with him. "She walked me home to my rooming house on several occasions because she was afraid I'd never make it on my own."

All gatherings took place among the sculptures. Works in various stages of completion were taken for granted as an accepted part of the background—carvings, clay work wrapped in damp cloths, large figures encircled by wooden scaffolding.

Whether commissions were forthcoming or not, the Girls always had major work underway. It formed a sort of unwitting camouflage around their circumstances, so that their friends seldom knew whether this was one of the times when the Girls were almost destitute, or whether their finances were in reasonable shape. The only indication of difficult times might be an unusual simplicity in the refreshments, but as guests often brought along contributions, even this was not particularly noticeable.

One of the principal facts of life in the Church was the omnipresence of animals. Especially cats and dogs. Most people remember the studio as being quite overrun with cats, and wonder how it was possible for the rats to have made any headway. And then they remember the sleekness of the cats, and their wonder ceases; the cats were too well fed to hunt. They led a privileged life. They even had a private entrance through a window on one side of the lower fireplace. One of them was always appearing like a ghost behind the frosted glass, and pushing his way in through the hinged pane. He would drop down onto the bench below, or onto the table, for that matter, and then proceed to the most comfortable seat available.

Neighbours' cats came to visit, and to have their kittens—usually in the best chair. It was difficult for regular visitors to be as enthusiastic about the cats as were the Girls themselves.

"We have trained those cats never to touch a bird!" Florence claimed. Perhaps the generous feedings helped.

Frances pressed a special guest to stay for lunch. "Where in blazes is that cold chicken that was put away from last night, Florence?" she called up from the kitchen in the basement. Oh, that chicken? Two hungry cats had come by that morning and looked beseechingly at Florence from the steps in the well outside the kitchen window.

Then there was the dog, Delilah, large and vaguely Airedale. The same Delilah who had protested against a surfeit of bagpipes. She had outlived a Samson of the same indefinite species as herself. She threatened to outlive them all. "The most horrible dog you could ever meet!" friends remember.

Delilah was inclined to snap. She was always where one was about to sit. It was necessary to move very carefully around Delilah. She was definitely the daughter of the house, and as such exacted due respect. She was never disciplined. One day a neighbour walked by in a new fur coat. Delilah took exception to it and rushed out, barking, to grab the fur and tear it. Florence and Frances placed great value on their neighbour, but her value counted for little compared to the worth of Delilah.

"Serves her right," the Girls said. "No one should wear a coat made out of all those dead animals!"

"When Delilah died," said A. Y. Jackson, who was not the animal's friend, "some of us thought we ought to have a banquet to celebrate."

Concern or compassion for the oppressed, the unfortunate, the derelict, man or beast, was a way of life at the Church. The Girls' extreme generosity, even when they had nothing themselves, was well known. As a result, a self-fulfilling line of artists and other people down on their luck found their way to the door of the Church.

Like the Italian fruit vendor who used to call there every Saturday afternoon.

It was during the depression and the times were desperate. The vendor quickly learned to make his final call of the week at the Church. Florence and Frances would buy everything that was left on his cart, much of it inedible after a week's picking over, and then they would invite him to stay for a hot meal. This weekly financial drain was rather serious, because the Girls' income was next to nothing at the time.

"We *must*." They were adamant when their friends voiced their concern.

When the Italian consul in Toronto persuaded the vendor to return to Italy, passage paid, as a conscript for Mussolini's army, their friends considered his repatriation a positive act of humanity on the part of Mussolini.

The Church took on its final form in the early 1950's. The Girls had come into a fair sum of money just prior to that time (not from their sculpture, but from investment in a modest gravel deposit on a rundown country property, bought years before against the sage advice of those who knew about such business matters). The money paid for a wing which was built onto one side of the Church, so that at last they could have separate studios. As Florence was by then over seventy years of age, it was an incredible act of optimism, though quite characteristic.

Someone once asked the Girls if they found that, by working so closely together, they unconsciously influenced one another's work.

"Never!" said Florence. "Frances and I could be modelling side by side, working from the same life-model, and the resulting figures would always be completely different interpretations."

"In fact," put in Frances, "we influence each other's work in contrary ways. I come in and suggest that Florence do this or that, and she always does the opposite."

"Maybe that's why she suggests it!" Florence retorted.

Their questioner persisted. Did they not find that, in sharing a studio, they tended to rub the sharp edges off each other?

Florence demurred. "No, we don't interfere with each other. We do our own work, and if we want the other fellow's opinion we ask for it. And sometimes we learn from it."

"We don't force our opinions on each other," Frances added. "And we mind our own business."

"Something that's nice to learn," said Florence, closing the issue.

Once the new wing was added, Frances was centred in the Church proper. Florence occupied the new addition, overlooking the tangled garden where she spent so many happy hours digging and encouraging things to grow (with rather too much success).

Their one splurge over the years—perhaps the only indulgence they had ever allowed themselves—was for something that no one else would have dreamed of coveting.

"Excavate below the entire building? Whatever for?" Their friends were slow to relinquish the comfortable relief that, with the proceeds from a substantial commission, the Girls would be financially secure for a while.

"Why, it will be excellent for storing lumber and chunks of wood for carving. We have it lying around all over the place now," they answered.

A $2000—storeroom it was.

Whimsical? Eccentric? Improvident? Doubtless they were. Yet they were absolutely solid as people and as artists. Throughout their forty-eight years in the Church, throughout the changing generations of artists, their basic beliefs remained positive and constant.

"The development of self as a whole goes into your work. But it takes work. Work—work—work," Frances said.

The Church saw them through all the ups and downs of the struggle for survival in the world of sculpture. Even towards the very end, when both were old, and partially crippled, and certainly forgotten in the more sophisticated shifts of artistic taste, one elemental fact remained. They were sculptors.

"Work is life. I hope to die standing at work," Florence told an interviewer on her eightieth birthday.

CHAPTER

I

———

Curiously enough, these two people whose names were synonymous with the growth of Canadian sculpture were not of Canadian origin. Florence Wyle and Frances Loring both came to this country from the United States.

On November 24, 1881, at Trenton, Illinois, a son and daughter— in that order of importance—were born to Solomon B. Wyle and Libbie A. Sandford.

Their father was a small-town chemist of farming stock, a strange character who reared his family with a heavy Victorian hand. When Florence and her twin brother were three years old, he proposed to move his family from Trenton. The story goes that he considered two towns before making his choice. One town boasted nine pubs and one church; the other, Waverly, offered nine churches and one pub.

Waverly it was.

Mr. Wyle was a person of strong and somewhat unusual persuasions. He insisted, for instance, that man was the only species capable of sleeping on its back, that the lower animals slept on their sides. Therefore his children were to sleep on their backs, as their superior development dictated. And he rose in the middle of the night to check that his edict was not overlooked. The enforced position was absolute torture for Florence.

Although her Father's puritanical and ascetic approach to life was akin to Florence's own nature, his rigid severity may indeed have been the beginning of her deep-rooted distrust of men. By the time she had reached womanhood, she could have been taken as the prototype of a feminist.

For Florence very early developed a sense of the inequalities of women's opportunities. She often recounted how her father would instruct her twin brother Frank to dig the garden or cultivate the flower beds, or some such task. When he returned home in the evening the job would be done, and Mr. Wyle would say, "Fine job, Frank!" Actually, Frank would not have touched a spade or a hoe. A baseball bat more likely. No sooner would his father have left the scene than Frank, enjoining Florence to do his chore, would be off to join his teammates. His sister could always be depended upon to cooperate.

"But, Florence," a close friend protested in later years, "you shouldn't have let Frank get away with it."

"Oh," she answered, "I didn't do it because I was covering up for Frank. I did it because I loved to work in the garden and hated housework. If I'd told on him, Father would have relegated me back to the house, 'where I belonged.'"

A photograph of Florence as a child of five or six reveals important clues to her make-up. It shows a little tomboy, hair spiking out in defiance of feminine tradition, sheltering a rooster protectively under the arm. The rooster had been found with a broken leg, and Florence, committed already to the broken and helpless, put a splint on the fracture. She kept the bird in a box just outside the kitchen door—"where I could get to him if he needed help." The leg healed, and after that, "he used to come and wait for me on the doorstep." He was the first of scores of creatures that she mended and befriended.

But there was more to the episode. As Florence watched over the rooster, afraid he might not recover, she asked a child's questions about sickness and dying. And at that tender age she was forced to a serious and enduring conclusion: "I stopped believing in God when they told me that animals didn't go to heaven."

As an old woman, trying to remember how she had first become interested in sculpture, she mused, "I think I was interested in life— trees and animals and such things—and I watched them, and I thought about them. And now and then I'd see a drawing of a bird or something and I'd connect things together."

But art as a means of livelihood was scarcely to be taken seriously in a home where hard, honest work was held in highest esteem.

When Florence finished high school in 1900, her father, with his stern sense of just obligation, gave her $500 to establish herself in life. She had long felt drawn to medicine, and accordingly, enrolled in the pre-medical course at the University of Illinois, with every intention of becoming a doctor. How she made ends meet after her initial year, with no further financial help from her family, she never explained. Her excellent academic mind undoubtedly marked her for any student jobs in the school's medical laboratories, and she always remembered with genuine gratitude the encouragement she received from her professors, but they must have been difficult years.

In the first year, her course included anatomical drawing, under Newton A. Wells; in the second year, painting; and in the third, sculpture. It was a logical, and for Florence, a happy development. "When I got into sculpture, I knew that was for me."

Apparently her art instructor thought so too. With his active encouragement, she transferred to the Chicago Art Institute in 1903. And so began her true life's work. One can only speculate how a modest, God-fearing, small-town family at the turn of the century reacted to this unheard-of step by their daughter. Plainly, the shift in interest widened the gulf that already separated Florence from her family.

At the Art Institute she excelled in sculpture from the very beginning. Her course was under the direction of Laredo Taft—"The Master," as he preferred to be called. Taft was rather a pedestrian sculptor who always managed to gather able people around him. Promising students soon found themselves promoted to working on details of Taft's own large figures. Florence was often requested, somewhat as an honour, to model hands and feet for his various works.

She was soon working day and night—studying in the daytime and assisting in teaching the evening classes. When she took over as instructor in the Saturday morning childrens' classes, she was actually supporting herself from her work—however meagrely. Taft, who was obviously very pleased with his new protégée, undoubtedly passed the employment her way. However, as master and protégée came to know one another better, relations cooled. Taft felt that he was entitled to certain "droits de maître"—a playful pat on the knee, the odd pinch on the bottom; Florence refused to accord him these rights. Her disenchantment with Taft was complete when an Indian head she had modelled in class disappeared, to turn up later incorporated into one of The Master's sculpted monuments erected in Washington.

Charles Mulligan, who taught her marble cutting, was an entirely different story. Florence was very reticent about the affair even as she looked back on it in later life. She definitely regarded her relationship with Charles Mulligan as a love affair, and it would seem, one of some depth and duration. But, like most of her early private life, she considered it just that—private. Whatever one might like to know about the involvement, all that is known is that it ended, unhappily yet apparently without rancour. Sixty years later, looking at his photograph which she had kept all the while, she spoke of him remotely as "a fine fellow."

Again Florence's experiences as a young artist confirmed and strengthened her belief that women had a few strikes against them as females in a male-ordered world, and especially in a traditionally male field. During her senior years at the Art Institute a group of officials from one of the southern states had seen and admired some of her work. They wrote to the Institute requesting the name and address of the artist, holding out the strong possibility of commissioning some sculpture. After they received word that the artist was a woman, they said they were terribly sorry, but they could not risk the commission; a woman might be unable to carry the work to completion. This kind of prejudice reinforced her uneasy distrust of men and male attitudes.

She was not, however, without honour in her field. While still at the Institute, she received the distinction of having a fountain in low relief purchased by the Art Museum of Chicago.

So matters rested in 1907, when Frances Loring arrived at the Chicago Art Institute as a student.

In contrast to Florence, Frances Loring came from a fairy-tale childhood—from a family who valued cultural achievement, a family who prized their women. Unlike Florence, Frances grew up knowing that women were fascinating, superior creatures.

Her father, Frank C. Loring, was a descendant of John Howland, who had been a passenger on the *Mayflower*. His father, who was agent in Chile for the family's Boston-centred shipping business, was also the United States' consul in Valparaiso. Frank therefore spent much of his childhood abroad. When he grew up he became active in mining back in the United States, and it was while he was involved in a mining venture in Indiana that he met and married Charlotte Moore. A son, Ernest, was their first born. Frances Norma Loring was born on October 14, 1887, while her father was in the midst of a further undertaking in Wardner, Idaho. When she was five years old, the family moved to a large, turreted house in Spokane, Washington.

By 1899, after a highly successful probe in the silver fields of British Columbia, Frank Loring felt ready to tackle Wall Street. He moved his wife and children to Washington D.C., then on to Europe the following year. They were no sooner there when the stock market teetered and crashed. Frank Loring lost everything.

"My father took a job that paid him $80 a month, and that was enough to keep him alive at home and us alive in Europe," Frances recalled later. He was unable to bring his family home for seven years.

Frances was thirteen years old and living in Geneva when she first came in contact with sculpture. She had shown no early talent in this direction, beyond an above-average skill in modelling mud pies. In Switzerland, a friend who was taking an art course gave her a piece of clay to play about with. "I defy anyone to take a piece of clay and play with it and not want to do sculpture!" Frances always claimed later.

Her next step was to persuade the Ecole de Beaux Arts in Geneva to let her study sculpture exclusively, and not bother with drawing or perspective or anything else that was part of the standard art course. (She later came to feel that she would have been better off not to have had her own way. "But I was a wilful youngster.")

Although Frances' first efforts at modelling did not reveal any signs of outstanding ability, she kept at it obstinately, and eventually convinced her dubious parents that she should begin serious art studies. Living comfortably enough in modest pensions in Switzerland, Germany and France, Frances studied art and Ernest engineering. In spite of the family's serious financial problems, in later life she recalled no impressions of hardship. They were simply in Europe and could not get back. She and her brother spent idyllic summers cycling on the quiet roads of the Continent, visiting en route most of Europe's great art.

Her working days while at school showed no trace of Bohemian influence. "I just worked all day as hard as I could work." Her parents insisted on special academic instruction in the evenings, "so that I could at least write in English and not disgrace the family." (Needless to say, she spoke fluent German and French.) Religious instruction along the way consisted of being taken to various churches where fine speakers were known to grace the pulpit. The art made a more lasting impression than the sermons.

Frances returned to America in 1907, the family coffers being somewhat replenished. She was twenty years old, vivacious, and extremely handsome. And still fired to study sculpture. She enrolled at the Chicago Art Institute where Florence Wyle was working and instructing. The two differed in aspect and in almost every other respect, except in their single-minded devotion to sculpture. They "clicked" immediately.

Meanwhile, Frances' father had moved his interests to the developing mining scene near Cobalt, Ontario. He was to become one of the pioneer mining engineers in the North, and throughout the rest of his life enthusiastically proclaimed Canada as the land of opportunity. Following the year in Chicago, Frances spent the summer months with her family at the mining headquarters in the wilderness. Her mother, making a quick adaptation from life in the capitals of Europe, had set up permanent housekeeping in commodious tents furnished with large carpets and traditional chairs and sofas. In this unlikely setting, amid the rough surroundings of the silver mines, the Lorings dressed for dinner, as befitted cultured people. Florence Wyle joined them as a summer guest, and was welcomed as a steadying influence on their own wilful artist.

The following year, 1908, Frances studied at the Academy of Fine Arts in Boston, before coming to Toronto to set up a temporary studio on King Street, across from the King Edward Hotel. She modelled the head of a violinist which was entered in the 1909 Ontario Society of Artists exhibition, held down the street in a building next to the old Princess Theatre. There was a fire, the exhibit burned, and the insurance money constituted Frances' first sale.

Moving on to New York, Frances took a studio on top of the Atelier Building in Union Square. By the following year, 1911, Florence managed to sever ties in Chicago and joined her in New York.

Their next stop was more than even the Lorings were prepared to accept: Greenwich Village. Frances' mother wept and pleaded with her daughter not to go. It was a labyrinth of wild Bohemian orgies. Her father blustered and threatened. To no avail. The art atmosphere of the Village beckoned irresistibly. Go they must, and go they did. They found living and studio space at 6 MacDougal Alley, in the heart of it all. And they worked and studied at the Art Students' League. The price of their move was high, however, in terms of pride, for in spite of their lofty defiance, the two girls found themselves forced to accept help from Mr. Loring in order to maintain the studio.

One of their early experiences in New York was most unpleasant; it would have sent lesser young ladies scurrying for home. They approached the well-established sculptor, French, in hopes of being taken on as studio assistants. With their training and experience they expected, reasonably enough, to be welcomed in a busy, overworked studio. Not so. French was mystifyingly brusque. It was not until some time later that they learned that Laredo Taft, still nursing his bitterness toward Florence, self-persuaded that she had not fully appreciated all he had done for her, had written French warning him that Florence and Frances were not only inconsequential sculptors but a couple of Lesbians to boot. It was their first brush with this innuendo.

Both Florence and Frances worked with great energy in MacDougal Alley. By 1913 they had turned out an impressive number of major works. Inspiration came from a variety of sources—from books, from memory, from their immediate surroundings: the rubber raincoat of a New York traffic policeman, for example. Frances found the garment remarkably sculptural in form. But how to get hold of a rubber-raincoat mounted policeman who was willing to model? She compromised by arranging for the neighbourhood grocer's horse to be brought around to pose for her in the alley outside the studio. Imagination and memory supplied the details. When finished she managed to persuade a New York bronze foundry to put out a limited edition of the figure, at their own expense—a practice that was not unusual at the time. The firm was to collect on the figures when they were sold. She had the satisfaction of seeing one figure cast in bronze, but while it was shown in a number of places, it was never sold, and in the end it was retained by the factory.

A poem by Edgar Allen Poe was her point of departure for the plaster model of a "Dream within a Dream." She interpreted the poem as a young girl standing on a shore clutching the grains of the sand of life in her cupped hands. They creep through her fingers, to the deep, "While I weep, while I weep." Years later the figure was carved in marble.

Florence was meanwhile putting a good deal of effort into an ambitious fountain group, "The Rites of Spring," which featured a large virile-looking angel. It was considered to be a splendid work. Unfortunately it survives only in photographs.

In between larger compositions, "to keep their hand in," the girls took turns sitting for one another's portraits.

The New York interval, in spite of continuing opposition from home, lasted until part way through 1913. Those were exciting times in New York, especially in art, and particularly in painting. (Nineteen thirteen was the year of the Armory Show, which sensationally shifted the direction of American painting.) Florence and Frances came to know people like Georgia O'Keefe. And they began to have a trickle of sales.

During a coincident lull in sales and inspiration, Frances was persuaded to go to Denver to visit her father's sister, and Florence went off in some other direction—possibly back home. In their absence from MacDougal Alley, Mr. Loring, who had not and would not become reconciled to the Greenwich Village experiment, went to New York and closed down the studio.

The move was effective and final. Frances came shortly afterwards to Toronto, ostensibly to care for her mother. Incredibly, father and daughter survived the outrageous action in New York. Perhaps to make amends to Frances and Florence, perhaps to induce his daughter to remain in Toronto, Mr. Loring offered to finance a modest working studio for the two of them. And so Frances and Florence came to the studio over the carpenter's shop. The Girls had arrived on the Toronto scene.

What was the principal attraction that led the Girls to settle permanently in Canada?

"Youth!" Frances said simply.

And for her it was as simple as that. She had been infected by her father's enthusiasm for a young country. The pioneer challenge—the adventure of breaking new ground.

Such external conditions did not significantly affect Florence's choice of residence. Sophisticated atelier or rough frontier, it mattered not, as long as she was free to work.

Pioneers they certainly were. According to the *Women's Saturday Night* in June of 1914, there were only three women sculptors on the entire Canadian scene: Florence, Frances and Winnifred Kingsford, who had studied in Paris under Bourdelle and had exhibited at the Paris Salon. When the Girls first knew her, she was working in Toronto in a studio on Adelaide Street. "The salt of the earth," was how they always described her.

Male sculptors were scarcely more in evidence. Walter Allward, the highly successful creator of inspired monumental works, was centre front on the Toronto stage. Emmanuel Hahn was in the wings. And there was only a handful of competent professional people working in Quebec—Hébert, Laliberté, Suzor-Coté.

The painting scene was livelier. The Group of Seven was beginning to let fly the sparks that reinterpreted and transformed Canadian landscape. The resistance and antagonism they experienced, or in some cases (more infuriatingly) the stony apathy, only served to make them dig in their heels with stubborn determination.

Frances and Florence, although friends and champions of the men who formed the Group, were not kindled by their revolutionary sparks. "We had settled into our point of view before we came in contact with the Group."

The hand-hewn rafters of the attic studio on Church Street vibrated with the hum of intense activity. Armatures took shape, clay was mixed, figures formed. Frances made one of her finest works at this time—"The Hound of Heaven." Once again it was a poem that had touched off the inspiration. "But it is not an illustration of Francis Thompson's poem," she said. "The poem simply put me in a certain rhythmic mood." She interpreted this mood with the figure of a woman—a person fleeing her conscience—and set up a moving and powerful rhythm through a Rodinesque sinuousness of surface. It was over fifty years before the piece sold.

Florence began work on a figure that she called "Rebirth." It conveyed the spirit of a man who had been knocked down by life but was getting to his feet again. "It can always be done," she insisted, firm in her faith in the individual's innate capabilities of regeneration. The model who posed for the study was a beautifully-built Englishman. In disconcerting contrast to the upright theme, he relaxed between poses by walking around on his hands. Naked, of course.

When Florence and Frances were settled in their new quarters they began to think about sending for the bulk of their sculpture, which had been left behind in storage in New York. Their inquiries forced them to a difficult choice: they could either scrape together every last cent they could find to pay the cost of packing and shipping their sculptures, or they could simply write off their lost works as experience and use their meagre funds to buy material for new. They opted for the future, for the surge of new ideas to be shaped in sculpture. (The earlier pieces were eventually sold at an auction by the storage people.) Their one real and lasting regret was the loss of the fine angel fountain by Florence.

It was well that they had their ideas and faith to sustain them, for their financial sustenance was practically nil. "I don't think many people would ever be sculptors—go into sculpture as a profession—if they realized what lies ahead of them once they're in it," Frances maintained later.

They survived, somehow, when many others did not.

25

Their work was exhibited with both the Ontario Society of Artists and the Royal Canadian Academy. Apart from the distinction (which nourishes the spirit, admittedly, but does little to feed the body), some practical benefits accrued. Their sculpture was seen and admired by members of allied professions. The architect John Pearson, for instance, began directing small commissions toward them. There were some enlarged coins to be made for the banking room of the Canadian Bank of Commerce. Not very interesting work, but it meant they could eat. Through Pearson, Florence was commissioned by the Albany Club to sculpt a relief portrait of the Prime Minister, Robert Borden. It was a start.

Their studio on Church Street was a delightful place to live and work. Their quarters were flooded with light from a number of great, deep windows, and there was good space and height for working. An open fireplace and walls lined with books gave a hospitable glow. But whatever the charms inside the studio, outside there was a most disreputable neighbourhood. Every once in a while there would be someone at the door downstairs, wanting to "speak to Rose." Rose was evidently a lady of the oldest profession who had occupied the quarters before the Girls.

"You damn fool!" Florence once said, when propositioned on the street.

None of this really bothered the Girls. With cheery disregard of tales of local murders, they continued to walk their two dogs each evening in the neighbourhood churchyards of St. James' Cathedral and the Methodist Church.

What bothered them, rather, was the attitude of the more respectable citizens of Toronto. The refined stratum of society was less than enthused by the entrance of these two unusual young women on the local sculpture stage. Quite to the contrary. How odd to have come to Toronto for such a strange enterprise as sculpture! And two women, mark you. For the second time, there was a distasteful implication. In Frances' words, "They thought it a peculiar thing that two young women should live together." The Girls dismissed it all with easy disdain. "You can't go through life worrying about what the public's going to think of you."

With the city's artists it was a different story. Walter Allward was one of the first to offer them hospitality, and in the early period they were invited to his home on Walker Avenue fairly frequently. Allward himself was a very successful sculptor by this time, although he had yet to do his most famous work—the Vimy Memorial in France. Strangely enough, his interest was purely social; it did not extend to helping the Girls establish themselves professionally. "He was a very self-absorbed man. A fine man, but not interested in promoting other people," remembered Frances, who admired his work tremendously. "But," she speculated, "he may not have believed in us enough."

A. Y. Jackson was one of the earliest visitors to the studio and became a fast, lifelong friend. Fred Varley came as well. "Varley was a fire—he was burning up, always," they said, attempting to describe the blazing talent that was in him. Florence tried to convey the fire that glowed in his eyes when she later modelled his portrait. He owed a good many meals to the Girls' hospitality, and when the great day arrived that he sold his first painting, he took the two of them out to dinner.

Then there was Robert Flaherty. "Don't start us on him, or we'll go on for hours," the Girls would say when asked about their old friend.

Flaherty was a complex man of extreme sensitivity and talent and possessed of the wildest impulses. At periodic intervals, and always unexpectedly, he would explode out of the northland and burst onto the Toronto scene. On occasion he would practically buy out a whole delicatessen and flower shop and would turn up at the studio with the booty. "You'd feel as though a whirlwind had struck you," Frances commented later.

Once, striking civilization after a length of time in the North, Flaherty invited the Girls to join him for dinner down at the old Queen's Hotel, where he was staying. When the Girls arrived at the hotel, there was no sign of their host in the unusually silent lobby. They waited and waited. At last a boy appeared with the message that Mr. Flaherty would be down in a minute. After a further considerable wait he did indeed appear, looking very white and very washed out.

"I've been in the bathtub trying to sober up," he explained. "I determined today that I was going to get the entire Queen's Hotel tight, and I've succeeded." Every cook, every waitress, every bell-boy.

Flaherty had gone up to the far North in the first place to look at iron ore property for Sir William MacKenzie. It was while on this exploration trip in 1914 that he came upon Belcher Islands in Hudson Bay, which he subsequently mapped. However, he became so much more interested in the native people than in the iron ore, that his course was set on a new tack. He developed a great love and admiration for the isolated and primitive Eskimos, with whom he seemed able to generate a mutual empathy. The result was his famous film, "Nanook of the North." Sadly, he found little backing for his work in Canada, and was forced to move his filming operations to the United States. His documentaries were marvellous expressions of his original, impetuous, creative spirit, but despite critical acclaim, they were box office failures. "A brilliant demonstration of the axiom that art doesn't pay," the *New Yorker* declared when he died in the early fifties.

According to Frances, he left a positive part of himself among the simple people that he loved. He was a fair man with a long nose and very blue eyes. For a time it was said in the North that whenever you saw a blond Eskimo with a big nose and blue eyes, his name was Flaherty.

"Robert was a grand person, but would have been hell to live with," Frances asserted. "Heaven help anyone to whom he meant a great deal—because you'd have to take him with terrific humour."

The Girls worked on. Exhibiting when and where possible. Limping along gamely on the proceeds from small, unimportant jobs. Gradually, larger, more hopeful prospects appeared.

Eric Brown of the National Gallery in Ottawa began to show a particular interest in their abilities. He was a man who did not hesitate to promote people he was interested in, and when work developed for sculptors through the War Records Organization in 1918, he directed a major commission to Florence and Frances. It was their first real break—overdue but gratefully accepted.

The project, one of a series of art works commissioned to stimulate the Canadian war effort—and from which sculpture had hitherto been excluded—consisted of a number of small bronze statuettes depicting women's work in the war. Florence modelled eight figures, and Frances six, among them, "The Munitions Worker" and "The Rod Turner." They were considered to be very fine examples of the Girls' work, and quickly received critical recognition. Financial consideration was slower in coming. The arrangement called for the various works to be purchased by an organization backed by Lord Beaverbrook, and then presented to the National Gallery. Eric Brown and the Gallery's president, Sir Edmund Walker, were responsible for choosing and dealing with the artists; Beaverbrook handled the purchasing of the art works. Unfortunately, once he got into the swing of the project, Beaverbrook over-extended himself and asked for more paintings and sculptures than there was money in the fund. The Girls had to wait two years before there was a financial settlement.

In 1918, Frances Loring affirmed her belief in the young country by becoming a naturalized Canadian citizen. Florence decided against it; at the time she happened to be disgusted with some government policy or other, and in any case, she would not cut the formal bond with the land of her birth.

Although Florence's work had generally been considered the stronger of the two—as verified in journalistic references—Frances found herself becoming more and more involved in designing and sculpting extensive series of memorial monuments for various communities. It was one of those fortuitous situations where a person's true *métier* seeks him out. Frances Loring and monumental sculpture. They were a match for one another.

"She doesn't like to do pieces unless she has to climb a ladder to get at them," Florence was moved to observe.

The memorials were a particular satisfaction for her because they afforded the opportunity to experiment in monumental concepts. And, of course, once set up, they were on permanent public view. There was also personal satisfaction in outwitting the commercial competition. Frances actually quite relished the preliminary skirmishings for contract position.

The St. Stephen, New Brunswick memorial was a case in point.

The issuing of contracts for war memorials was stacked against sculptors because of serious competition from the granite concerns. They claimed the war memorial market because of their experience in tombstone manufacture. For them it was simply a case of enlarging the product. (Which accounts for the many mounds of granite atrocities, misnamed war memorials, that defile city squares.) It was the practice of these concerns to have someone representing their interests unobtrusively placed on the various memorial committees. Rumour has it that they even donated sums of money to the cause if their man was named to the committee. Sculptors innocent in the ways of business were no match in that sort of game.

Frances, with shrewd impetuosity, decided to give battle with her own weapons: the art of her work and the force of her personality. When word came of a memorial for St. Stephens, she got busy and made a splendid model of a young soldier sorrowing for his lost comrades, a cross at his feet, his rifle silent. She packed it in a cereal box, put the box under her arm, and caught a train for New Brunswick. Once in St. Stephens she contacted the committee chairman, Arthur Gagnon. He admired the artistry of the maquette and the sincerity of its expression. He was even encouraging about its being approved by the committee. Being an observant man, he was well aware of the vulture-like interest in the project by the local granite concern, which had been scooping up the memorial commissions in the entire region. And, being a shrewd man, he was prepared for their tactics.

The maquette, or scale model, came before the appointed official body—presented by Frances herself. The granite people had their man there as well, an Irishman who specialized in making people weep. After a heart-rending tribute to "our poor lost boys," he would whip out the contract to be hastily signed by the weeping committee members. On this occasion the drama was enacted on schedule. The contract was laid before the group. And then the chairman cleared his throat. "Let's wait until morning to sign this," he suggested. By the time morning came, reaction had set in—and Frances got the job.

Florence, meanwhile, had not been idle. Once the War Records efforts were out of the way, she forged ahead with figures like "The

Key"—a fine lyrical sculpture of a young woman holding a symbolic key. Florence was very highly regarded by her fellow artists, although her trickle of private sales, while in their way as important, did not raise the same kind of public ripple as her partner's more spectacular enterprises did. Obviously a pattern was being set, a balance struck between the quiet but fervent dedication of Florence Wyle's approach to her work, and the flamboyant drive of Frances Loring's total involvement. The contrast acted as a built-in stabilizer for both of them. Those who could not see the balance, betrayed their lack of perception in trivial ways: the order of their names, for example. Although one was seldom considered without the other, they were collectively referred to as the Loring-Wyles, never the Wyle-Lorings. Such matters did not concern the Girls; each recognized the other's particular worth.

A photo taken of the Girls around this period by their friend Flaherty shows them to have been unusually handsome young women, in contrasting ways. Frances Loring had a dark, sensuous, Mediterranean elegance sharpened with high intelligence. Florence Wyle had a more delicate, classic beauty lit by an almost child-like innocence which was part of the sensitivity and purity that was her strength. Small wonder that the local police chief instructed his men to keep them under a protective eye. Small wonder, too, that their complete immersion in their work was now and again interrupted by romantic complications.

For Frances the most serious interruption occurred during the early years in Ontario. Once again Mr. Loring felt called upon to step in decisively and face a head-on collision with his impulsive daughter. This time it was to put his foot down on Frances' romantic involvement with a young German—a most unacceptable match, viewed against the background of a nation at war with Germany. He came into and went from her life before she had made close ties in Toronto, so that friends of later years knew nothing of him. But memory of the affair remained within the family as a sort of myth. Frances herself was a very old woman before she confided to two or three intimates that he had been the love of her life, and that after he had gone, all other men paled in comparison. She conceded that he had been somewhat irresponsible, not at all traditional hus-

31

band material, but she reflected in her old age, perhaps she had made a tragic mistake by not throwing everything to the wind and eloping with him to the States. She certainly did not forget him. Much later, when a fellow sculptor was to visit a certain city in the States, Frances secretly requested her to find out how he was—what he looked like. "But," she added anxiously, "don't let Florence know I've asked!"

Florence was not exempt from male attention either. An architect had taken an office across the hall from the studio, a young married man, who nevertheless found many excuses to drop into the studio. It was not dangerous, really, as Florence was too busy to take undue notice of him. But his wife, having dropped by his empty office unexpectedly on two or three occasions, and having found him each time in the studio across the hall, ordered him to terminate his visits. Forthwith. Unhappily for the architect, Florence was working at that time with plaster of Paris. When his wife came by on yet another unannounced visit, a tell-tale series of white footprints, leading back and forth from office to studio, exposed the architect's failure to obey his wife's orders.

In short, life at the studio was colourful, and work was going strong. Yet there seemed no escape from the recurrent dreary problem—lack of funds. The war memorial commissions were slow in yielding actual cash and preliminary payments were ear-marked for materials necessary to get the projects underway. In desperation Frances grasped at the job of whipping up a plaster lioness and cubs to sit over the new Dufferin Gates at the Canadian National Exhibition. She modelled a lioness, and then one cub, from which five cubs were cast with the heads separate from the bodies. These were carefully arranged around the lioness with the heads fastened on the bodies at different angles. Florence and Winnifred Kingsford helped with the technical end of the job. All in all, it entailed about ten days of hectic work. The three of them were washing their hands behind the scaffolding as the mayor was dedicating the gate with its statue. While it was not a deeply satisfying undertaking, at least it paid a few bills.

In 1920, both Girls were elected to membership in the Ontario Society of Artists, and were made Associate Members of the Royal

Canadian Academy. In those days membership amounted to full professional recognition. Practical recognition was also forthcoming; they finally received payment for their War Records figures—$5,000 for fourteen works, from which the considerable costs of bronzing had to be deducted. The sum was not overwhelming, but it was opportune. Florence was not well and needed to get away to the country. "A real garden she could dig in," Frances explained.

They used part of their War Records money to buy a farm near the Rouge River. It was a wild run-down place that grew mostly poison ivy, a crop that Florence soon disposed of. She knew from childhood how to make a wonderful garden grow. "We had enough to eat, anyhow," she later acknowledged modestly.

There was a farmhouse on the property which they rented to friends. The Girls themselves took a little square shack up on the ridge overlooking the Rouge. There were one hundred and fifty acres altogether. "We only wanted to buy ten acres, but found it was cheaper to buy a hundred and fifty," they explained. Although for many years the farm had little value except as a welcome week-end retreat, ultimately it proved to be the closest thing to a fortune that ever came their way.

Later that same year the events occurred that forced them from their quarters over the carpenter's shop, and led them to their church on Glenrose Avenue. "Rather foolish to buy them both in the same year, but one came on top of the other." The mortgages for both properties stayed with them for years.

The Church was to be their studio, their centre, their home for the rest of their lives.

"You must get such satisfaction from being creative artists." "If only I had time to do a little clay modelling!" "Working in clay must be so relaxing."

Frances put such comments in their place.

"There's a vast difference between modelling in clay because you like it, and becoming an artist and devoting your life to it. You can model in clay because you enjoy it, and you will get nowhere. To get somewhere you have to work day after day after day on the same thing."

When they were asked how they had managed to carry on with sculpture in spite of financial pressure, she answered, "We have always stuck to things; that's the point. It's a case of if you want to do a thing you do it, hang it all."

Despite their close association, it was obvious that the distinctiveness of the Girls' personalities was indelibly reflected in their work.

Florence, the lover of purity and truth, expressed herself in classic forms. "The Greeks settled my ideas—gave them to me in the beginning. Greek sculpture; I think it's the best we've ever had."

While she based her designs on the discipline of anatomy, her figures were warmed and brought to life by a very personal sense of inspired lyricism. Instinctively she could touch the true nature of any subject, and then adapt it to the natural qualities of the material she was using. She had loved the beauty of the human figure since she had first encountered anatomy in her medical studies, and many of her sculptures were of nudes. "The human animal wears so many clothes that he hides his beauty. Idiotic. Especially in hot weather."

Frances on the other hand, was influenced by classicism, but even more by the vital and dramatic sculptural philosophy of Rodin and

Bourdelle. Doubtless inspired by the grand art she had seen as a young girl in Europe, she began to develop a sense of the monumental.

Florence Wyle worked quietly and privately on garden figures, portrait heads and plaques of people who interested her, not concerned with manoeuvring for commissions. In the same studio, using the same basic equipment, Frances Loring, on the brink of a remarkable public career, was working on monumental pieces which demanded not only Herculean labour from the sculptor, but also great diplomatic agility in dealing with people.

Although they were a seemingly disparate team, they were united in a sense of dedication to their art which rested on a basic reverence for life and human dignity.

During the early twenties a new, and previously elusive, element introduced itself, albeit briefly: they began to sell a few things. And Frances received more commissions for war memorials. One of these emanated from Augusta, Maine.

Augusta decided that it must have a replica of the memorial in St. Stephen. The situation was somewhat unusual: the man who was donating the money for it was not expected to live for another year, and the committee therefore wished to have the monument in place by the following eleventh of November. The matter could have been resolved by simply casting another bronze from the original plaster which was still at the foundry in Belgium. Except for an awkward technicality. The uniform and equipment of a U.S. soldier were considerably different from those of his Canadian counterpart. This demanded a complete reorganization of the figure. Since there was not nearly enough time to make a new figure, the inventive Frances proposed that she make the necessary changes by working with plaster of Paris directly on the original model. It seemed the ideal solution.

Accordingly, Frances made plans for the trip to Belgium. The unresolved item was the rifle the soldier was to hold. It had to be an authentic American rifle used in the war. Frances arranged for the United States government to send one ahead to Brussels. When she herself arrived, she found the issue being treated almost as an international incident. The Belgian government would allow no American arms into the country. The rifle had been embargoed at the port of entry. Frances rose to the diplomatic demands of the occasion, and her urgent entreaty resulted in permission for her to have the rifle for a couple of hours while she copied it in clay.

The sculpture was successfully remodelled, hastily cast, and loaded aboard ship. By a quirk of misfortune, however, the ship happened to be a tramp steamer which called in at several ports before finally docking at Boston. Frances rushed to receive the bronze, but no, it could not be unloaded in Boston because it was consigned for New York. Incredibly, stretching frustration to the breaking point, the ship was delayed by fog for three days outside New York harbour. When it finally docked, the statue was discovered to have been loaded under tons of Belgian glass which was destined for another port. The glass would have to be discharged before the ship could return to New York to unload the sculpture. No, no! There was no time. Please, a man's life was involved. Please, a whole town was waiting. The shipping company was finally persuaded; they agreed to shift the glass then and there. For $80.

The bronze was shipped that night by truck for Augusta, Maine. It arrived in the morning, was erected by eleven o'clock, and the unveiling ceremony began.

"I nearly went insane during that period," Frances said, recollecting the incident.

A number of other assignments followed in quick succession. First came the commission for a memorial in Galt, Ontario. It was unveiled with "lots and lots of bands." She remembered little else about the ceremony. "By the time you've finished a large work, you've worked so hard under great pressure to get it done in time that you don't really notice much about the unveilings."

Next came a war memorial for the Law Society of Upper Canada at Osgoode Hall. It was to be a carving in Carrara marble. The design took form as a symbolic figure of a youth who had shed the robes of everyday life to offer himself to the cause of humanity. Frances built up a full-size model, seven feet high, which was sent to Italy to be copied in marble by professional stone carvers.

People mistakenly assumed that because commissions such as this were for large figures, it followed that the sculptor received a large fee. Alas, not so. Frances was, without exception, underpaid. With the heavy expenses of casting, carving and transporting, a sculptor might even lose money unless he had a good business head. On several occasions Frances just got through by the skin of her teeth.

During this period of intense work activity, the Girls somehow found time to play matchmakers. In spite of their own romantic disillusionments, they decided to arrange a second marriage for Mr. Loring.

Frances' father had been widowed a few years earlier, and they felt he needed someone to look after him. Besides, he was now centred in Toronto and was underfoot more than was desirable in the busy sculpture studio. Accordingly, a party was arranged in the Church, which casually brought together a dozen spinsters and widows of the Girls' acquaintance—and Papa Loring. From this group of prospects the field was tactfully eliminated to three, and then to one, Miss Burns, whom Mr. Loring seemed to favour. How to move him from favour to proposal?

When the old gentleman was overheard to express himself as being partial to a certain type of fruit cake, declaring he might even marry the woman who could bake one, their question was answered. A scurrying among noted cooks within their group of intimates produced a suitable cake, which was passed off as the accomplishment of Miss Burns. Marriage followed shortly.

Without conscious effort and even at times in spite of themselves, the Girls began to attract a large circle of friends. When Barker Fairley, for instance, was brought to the studio by a mutual acquaintance in 1921, Florence, ever on her guard against men, announced out of the blue, "I'm forty years old!" But Barker liked both of the Girls immensely, and found that everything about them and the studio exuded warmth.

Most important among all their friends, was Keith. Keith MacIver was a native of the Hebrides Islands in Scotland. After a stint as a rubber planter in Malaya, and wartime years in Mesopotamia, he had come to Canada to visit his brother Robert, who was teaching Sociology at the University of Toronto. Deciding to stay awhile, Keith took a job with Canada Packers, where he was given to understand that there was opportunity for a man like himself to work up into a key position in the firm. All went reasonably well until the workers went on strike to protest terrible working conditions in the slaughter house and meat-packing plant. Feeling their cause to be just, Keith resigned in sympathy. Frances, problem solver *extraordinaire*, proposed that he join her father's mining enterprises in the north country.

From then on Keith became a part of the North. His self-endurance, cool-headed thinking and unfailing sense of humour enabled him to survive the wilderness. He roamed the North for years in search of minerals, enriching the mining interests of his associates and himself with the wealth of his experiences.

During the winter months he made his Toronto headquarters at the Church. It was inevitable that his presence there would be construed by some of the neighbours as "a man in the Girls' house." He was rather the man *about* the house—repairing, casting, chopping wood, making furniture. Later he took over the old Tom Thomson shack behind the Studio Building on Severn Street, and after reclaiming it from the encroachments of rot and decay, used it as his home base, much as Thomson had done. He married Edith Alexander, head cataloguer at the University of Toronto Library and another member of the Girls' intimate circle. A quiet, unassuming man of rare spirit, Keith was the Girls' closest and most trusted friend until his death in the mid-sixties.

These early years in the Church tested and proved the Girls' ability to maintain separate reputations and distinctive careers. Florence, for instance, while definitely the more retiring partner, was nevertheless chosen in 1924 as the only woman juror for the Canadian section of the famous Wembley show, a British Empire Exhibition held in Wembley, England. A photo of the jury shows Florence, the great manhater, sitting in warm camaraderie with the men who were the most respected painters in the country. A tremendous controversy broke around the issue of their selections when it became known that they had chosen the new work of such painters as the members of the Group of Seven. "Decadent," the reactionary factions labelled them.

Eric Brown managed to persuade the powers-that-be that the show must go to Wembley as planned. The bitter furor accelerated. There were letters to the papers, there were demands for Brown's resignation. If he had not been a man of great character and persuasively knowledgeable about painting, the show would never have left the country. He stood his ground, and Canada was represented at the exhibition.

Florence's position as a judge required her to go to Europe to attend the gala opening at Wembley. She looked forward to the trip with great excitement, especially to the possibility of finally getting to Paris. To her surprise, however, she found Paris disappointing. Perhaps because the city was still in its annual summer doldrums, perhaps because she had realized her dream too late. On the other hand, London, which had never figured in her American imagination, captivated her completely.

The Canadian exhibition, which had been under such bitter fire from its own countrymen, was an unqualified success at Wembley. In competition with a generally high-calibre display, the Canadian section stole the show. Will Ogilvie, who had recently arrived in England from South Africa, responded so positively to the fresh vigour and very personal expressions of the Canadians, that he set aside plans to study art in London in favour of seeking out the painting atmosphere in the country that had nurtured these vivid works. And so another distinguished artist was added to the Canadian scene.

Ironically, the triumph of the exhibition did not endear Eric Brown to the academic die-hards at home. At the first possible opportunity they launched a concerted campaign to oust him from his post at the National Gallery. But it was not so easy. A large sector of the artistic community rallied behind him—with the Girls in the thick of it all. Meetings were held night after night either in the Church or in the Studio Building, to hammer out manifestos, draft petitions, and so forth. They finally won the day, and Brown retained his post. Frances probably spoke for his many supporters when she said, "Eric Brown was more help to the artists than anyone else in Canada!"

Fortunately life was not always so serious. The Saturday-night parties were getting underway. They were not parties in the generally accepted sense; there was never any feeling that people were being "entertained." Rather, they were simply gatherings of friends. A heterogeneous collection of Canadian painters, writers, and musicians as well as alcoholic professors, out-of-work models, and other strays from various walks of life—all welcome at the Church. Singers might sing, violinists might play, poets might recite, but on the most informal basis. The Girls possessed an extraordinary ability to make people feel at home.

One evening Keith's prospecting partner, Pete Swanson, "the strongest man in the North" and the seventh son of a seventh son, decided to read teacups, which he could do with amazing accuracy. On this particular night he said to one of the men, "You're considering having an affair with a woman who looks like . . ." and he went on to describe in detail a woman he had never seen. Everyone present recognized her from his word picture. Even Frances was not sure whether Swanson had done some research or whether he just had an uncanny awareness.

Swanson would come down from the North starved for culture, but he always seemed to act like a bear in a salon. He attended one of Jeanne Dusseau's concerts at the Eaton Auditorium during one sojourn in the city. Unfortunately he had been celebrating rather too rigorously beforehand and jumped up at some climactic point, clapping and shouting, "Bravo!" much to the disgust of the rather staid audience. There was no teacup reading at the studio for some time after this display.

Although the Girls were still very attractive despite the passing years, they did not bother with fashions or make-up to enhance their looks. Florence recognized festivities by putting on an old velvet jacket. Frances, despite her expanding girth, could always manage to look striking and elegant by flinging a cape over her shoulder.

Gatherings in the Church were by no means predominantly art parties. Art groups met there to be sure, but there was also an enormous amount of music in the studio. Dusseau and her brilliant accompanist, Gwendolyn Williams, gave frequent musical evenings to a select group who were particularly fond of Dusseau's singing. They were musical happenings rather than structured concerts, with requests welcomed from the audience. The accompaniment was of necessity on the only available instrument—a terrible little upright piano that the Girls had been storing for somebody for years—but the acoustics in the vaulted Church were superb. John Goss, the English baritone, was often part of the group during his visits to America, as was Roland Hayes.

Florence, in particular, loved vocal music. And she herself once made a less-than-musical contribution to one of these events. During a pause in the performance she was pressed by a guest to explain more fully a previous reference to hog calling in Ohio, her home state. She responded by giving a spectacular call—an enormous sound from such a small person.

Will Ogilvie said once, of the Girls, "They have a wonderful sense of knowing how to live." This was fortunate in a practical sense, for when the demand for war memorials died, and the few people who wanted garden sculpture had already bought it, they went back to trying to manage on next to nothing.

"I'd be satisfied," a young and naive sculptor confided to them many years later, "if I could bring in $2,000 a year."

"Well, my dear," they said gently, "there have been many years when the two of us together didn't bring in $2,000."

In 1927 the anthropologist Marius Barbeau arranged for Florence and Anne Savage to go to Skeena River in northern British Columbia, to make models and drawings of the fast decaying totem poles still standing in the Indian villages bordering the river.

"Daring Canadian Girl in an Indian Village," ran the heading of a newspaper column upon Florence's return. "Miss Florence Wyle Models Totem Poles for Government." (A forty-six-year-old girl, daring or otherwise? How Florence must have chuckled!) With admirable but garbled fervour one paper reported, "Potash in Progress in Hagwilgel on her Arrival." The paper was doubtless referring to an Indian potlatch ceremony, held usually on some significant occasion such as when a new pole was erected.

The trip was a wonderful experience and Florence received great kindness from the Indian hosts. Her natural dignity and respect for her fellow human beings stood her in good stead as she sat modelling under the surveillance of the Indian families who owned the various poles.

41

Florence especially loved the unrestored poles—silver grey in colour, leaning at picturesque angles along the streets of the villages. One of the totems at Skeena Crossing, from which she modelled a delightful little owl, is still standing.

Frances was busy in a different sort of environment. She had gone to Italy to supervise the carving of the memorial for the Law Society of Upper Canada, which seemed to be a long time in the making. Her dealings with the Italian carvers were particularly frustrating. Although they were professionally competent, she despaired of their ever completing the figure. But after much prodding, the memorial was finished to her satisfaction, and was ultimately installed in place at Osgoode Hall.

The final payment was invested in a new car, "Osgoode," a Model-A touring car, which replaced "Susie," distinctly one of the oldest Fords in Toronto. Osgoode had problems, too, and required a great deal of cranking, but in comparison with Susie, it carried them back and forth from the country in great style. The Girls would take off for a week-end at the farm, car packed with food, and careen down the road with Samson and Delilah each leaning out a back window barking furiously. Frances always drove. She was an atrocious driver and left a path of destruction as she went—garbage cans, posts, whatever stood in her way. Florence was the navigator and the mechanic. If parts came loose she would fasten them back with haywire—a successful if unorthodox method. When the car was new, Frances was unsure of the brakes. As they headed down the Yonge Street hill south of St. Clair, Florence leaned out the window shouting, "Look out—we're coming!"

On the political front, Frances was becoming more and more involved in crusading for the art world. She was convinced that a great deal could be accomplished if artists could be persuaded to join forces and fight for themselves. The Eric Brown issue after the Wembley show strengthened her conviction. Things were slow in 1928, though, and she wrote to Brown, "Haven't any fighting in the offing this winter. Things seem very quiet."

This was soon remedied. Frances and Emmanuel Hahn went off to Montreal to meet with sculptor Henri Hébert to lay the framework of an organization "to promote closer cooperation among sculptors in Canada, and for the encouragement, improvement and cultivation of the art of sculpture."

As Frances and Hahn had always been sparring partners, the meeting in itself must have been lively. Both probably enjoyed the jousting. The discussions resulted in the founding of the Sculptors' Society of Canada. The charter members were Frances Loring, Florence Wyle, Elizabeth Wyn Wood, Emmanuel Hahn, Henri Hébert and Alfred Laliberté.

Although a formal charter was not taken out until 1932, the members consolidated their earlier action by whipping up enthusiasm among sculptors in general, so that in October of 1928 they were able to mount a show at the Art Gallery of Toronto, presenting 203 works of sculpture. Florence Wyle alone showed fifty-three works; Frances Loring thirty-three. It was a time of tremendous hope for the sculptors, and while the showing did not reap much financially, the gallery-going public had a chance to see their work. They were taking the advice of Frances, who often urged, "For God's sake, look at sculpture!"

CHAPTER

4

Not many people were looking at sculpture in the twenties, not even fellow artists. The reaction of the Girls' great friend Alex Jackson typified the interest of even those in allied arts. After he had been to an Academy exhibit, Jackson dropped in at the Church, enthusing about the paintings he had seen.

"Did you see any sculpture you were interested in?" Florence asked him.

"No," he answered with his usual honesty. "I didn't look at the sculpture."

Sculptors were faced with a disheartening public apathy, but their most immediate impasse was the wall of indifference from the painters, who made up the larger balance of membership in the art societies. Sculpture and sculptors were only an afterthought. At exhibitions sculpture was shoved into corners. (Small wonder the viewers passed it by.) It could not be allowed to take up valuable wall space; that was reserved for paintings. "They always managed to put the woodcarvings over the hot air radiators," Frances remembered with disgust.

"Sculpture is harmony of mass, as music is harmony of sound," Florence wrote. But rock and sun and lake and hillside was the language the painters understood. Form and line in clay or stone or wood was like a foreign tongue whose sounds and rhythm they may have admired, but whose meaning and pattern they never understood. Florence and Frances had many friends among the painters, but these friends stayed within their own idiom; they never learned the language of sculpture. They virtually ignored three-dimensional work.

"They don't see it," the Girls absolved them realistically.

Frances refused to accept the situation. Sculpture had the longest and most noble history of all the arts! Neither she nor her fellow professionals had any intention of allowing the small fire of public interest they had kindled to sputter and die. They would build up the fire and bypass the painters.

When the S.S.C. was formed, there were only the four members in the Toronto chapter: Loring, Wyle, Hahn and Wyn Wood. Hébert and Laliberté carried the banner in Quebec. Hahn took on the first tenure of presidency, while Frances was unanimously elected secretary—mainly because she had a typewriter and could speak French. Personality clashes were easily submerged in the common cause because of the members' respect for one another's work. The Girls, for instance, had immense admiration for the early work of Elizabeth Wyn Wood, in spite of periodic spats.

None of the six were in the least intimidated by their pitifully small representation. With the confidence of crusaders, they organized shows to bring sculpture before the public. Their efforts were more educational than remunerative, as it was most unusual for works to sell from shows. That would come later. What mattered was the show of sculpture. The exhibitions gave the public a chance to look at *sculpture* and offered despairing sculptors the substance of hope, made them feel their work was justified and necessary to the human cause. The society actively encouraged young sculptors to join them. Frances wrote letters to people like Eric Brown, inquiring about any up-and-coming young artists. Gradually the ranks of the S.S.C. began to swell and elicit respect.

Frances Loring had implicit faith in the constructive influence of the Sculptors' Society, and she worked tirelessly for its ends. She was one of those rare individuals who could fly into battle with whole-hearted resolve, vanquish her opposition with a volley of enlightened unorthodoxy, and emerge not only victorious, but carrying with her the trophy of her opponent's full respect. No intelligent individual tangled with her lightly, because it was too well known that the strength of her arsenal rested on ruthless sincerity, warmed by a penetrating wit and fired by unselfish motives. She battled for other sculptors, not for herself, even over personal issues. The combination made her position almost impregnable.

Florence Wyle was vitally concerned with the same issues, but for her, an artist's first duty was to his work; the battle for the recognition of the art of sculpture would ultimately be won by the integrity of the work itself.

Throughout the sculptors' struggle to establish a beachhead in the art world, the National Gallery added active support to their thrust. And not merely nominal support; the gallery gave real impetus through purchases from various sculptors. Frances' bronze "Derelicts" was bought from the Sculptors' Society exhibit of 1929, for example. Limited funds could provide only marginal assistance, but the gallery did what it could in a period when no one else thought it important.

Times were miserable. The Depression was looming, and it was not difficult to foresee that the sculptors, whose wares had little market value in the best of times, would be among the first victims. Ironically, the Girls, probably because of their established reputation, were assumed to be immune from the cares of struggling for professional survival. But artists do not live by inspiration alone, and even solid reputations do not buy material to transmute inspiration into tangible works of art. So the letter which arrived for Florence from the National Gallery, in February of 1931, was more than welcome. "The Trustees showed great interest in your woman's torso shown at the Sculptors' Society exhibition here and expressed their desire to have first opportunity of considering it again in the event of its being cut in stone or marble of a colour not unlike the plaster, which seems to suit it very well."

While the invitation appeared on the surface to be only a tentative possibility, there was elation in the studio. In its own cautious way, the National Gallery had issued what was tantamount to an unofficial commission. Its directors liked the figure, but wanted it in permanent material. Sadly, since times were lean for them as well, their letter omitted any mention of financial assistance to help the project toward fruition.

No one but an artist would have been demented enough to touch such a lame proposition. But the confirmed artist is also a confirmed gambler. From desperation, perhaps. Nothing ventured, nothing gained. A simple credo. The facts of life. Florence could stand her ground among veteran gamblers.

There she was, impoverished, with no immediate prospects, but quite willing to put herself in debt to initiate a project that offered no commitment other than "a first opportunity of considering." But what artist could resist the invitation to make his art permanent?

The "Torso" in question was an extremely beautiful figure. Perhaps more than in any other piece she ever made, Florence had achieved a total expression of her basic exuberance for life. This time her devotion to anatomy was skilfully subjugated to underline a statement of contained, rhythmic motion. The over-life-sized woman's figure throbbed with a life force—like a plant unfolding itself irresistibly and triumphantly to the world. How satisfying to have the marble represent her as part of the collection of the National Gallery! She did not hesitate.

Knowing that nothing further would develop until she produced the finished piece, the "Torso" was despatched to the stone cutter, who was apparently satisfied to accept the official interest in the commission as sufficient to make Florence a good credit risk. He was to copy the design in marble from the plaster original, using a mechanical copying device known as a pointing machine. Following the standard approach of the times toward carving, he would carry out all the preliminary rough heavy work, before returning it to Florence to finish.

As this additional debt was accumulating, the Girls were finding it extremely difficult to live. There was little cash to speak of coming into the Church. Infrequent dribbles from here and there. In a letter of rare reference to difficulties, Florence wrote to Brown in January of 1932, "We are awfully broke—even worse than usual."

Friends who had benefitted endlessly from the Girls' generosity, suddenly felt the need of lessons in sculpture. "Would you consider taking a small group of pupils?" Yes, the Girls would. But there was the delicate problem of payment. They refused a fee. Were these not their friends? Besides there was reason to suspect the seriousness of the group's interest. Somehow the lessons had more of the festive air of a social occasion than a sober study of sculpture. As a compromise, a hat was set out into which anyone who was able dropped a small sum. Food brought in by the students for supper afterwards served as a subtle ruse to get food into the studio larder without offending the Girls. It was absolutely taboo to mention or even pretend to notice the state of the finances.

Students of the smaller, more serious morning class felt the diminished effect of their money dropping into the hat when they heard shuffling steps approach the lower door of the Church. "There's Hardy," Florence would say with enthusiasm. "He's here for his breakfast." Hardy was a doddering down-and-outer who had started coming to the Church once a week to do janitorial work. As might be expected, he was always given a meal while he was there. Eventually he fell into the habit of coming around every morning for a bowl of porridge. The unfortunate man was an ex-sailor who had served in the merchant navy under another name, and confusion over his true identity complicated the matter of his eligibility for a pension. The Girls spent endless hours researching and unravelling the tangle, and eventually Hardy was awarded his pension. Meanwhile, he came around every morning for breakfast.

There was also the matter of Italian lessons. Throughout this period Frances and Florence were encouraging classes in Italian as a means of subsidizing their friend the Italian consul, who was riding out the Depression on a starvation allowance. All in all, it was a somewhat defeating experience to attempt to help the Church Girls.

In due course Florence's "Torso" was returned, carved to within a quarter-inch of the actual surface. It was ready for the final stage in its metamorphosis from maquette to full-sized clay study, to plaster cast, to finished marble. As warm weather approached, Florence decided to move it out to the studio at the farm, and finished it there in the summer of 1932. Purchase of the figure was approved by the National Gallery, but owing to a lack of funds, they did not pay for it until the following spring. Florence's letter to Eric Brown, written some time after the payment was finally made reveals their situation as they waited for the money.

"It has taken me this long to recover from the shock (but not to cash the cheque). It was very welcome indeed. I'm in the midst of an orgy of bill-paying. You wouldn't think there would be that many 'please remits' in the world."

The torso was one of the few sculptures that was worked on earnestly out at the Rouge shack. As Frances once put it, "When you get out in the country in the summer, you loaf."

They did have a bona-fide studio out there, though—one built onto the existing cabin. "We hammered and nailed it ourselves," they said proudly.

Frances often told the story of how, in the midst of construction, she was standing under the eaves, working away while Florence was up on the roof laying the tarpaper. The first thing Frances knew, she looked up and there was tarpaper, Florence and all rolling down the roof right over her head. "Fortunately she knew how to fall."

"Going to the farm" was the usual thing on summer week-ends for years. There was almost always company—a few regulars, with a sprinkling of occasionals, and even a few business people. Sometimes a whole art society would meet there for a picnic.

The shack had been a dilapidated tumbledown place when the Girls bought it, and it never was much better. A porch was added, the floor propped up and the roof patched, to make it liveable, but it always exuded an air of very dubious stability. Its charm rested in the general atmosphere of unquestioned relaxation. Inside, the furniture was unmentionable. Boards had been put together for benches and bedsteads, bits and pieces had been added from friends' attics. At one point an acquaintance kindly donated a lovely formal dinner set that she was replacing in her own home. She felt the dishes might be useful at the Rouge, but of course they were terribly out of place. The Girls sat around hating them for a time and then went back to using their chipped pie plates.

The shack housed many beds in varying stages of decrepitude—enough to sleep about a dozen people, necessarily of the sort who did not object to mouse holes in the blankets. Frances herself was awakened one night by an insistent tugging on her long braid which trailed from her cot onto the floor. A mouse was intent on dragging the prize home to his nest. House guests were safer on hot nights, for then the beds were hauled onto the roof of the porch.

Saturday picnickers would wander about, doing as they liked—

49

sketching, dawdling, collecting firewood, whatever. Then, toward evening, they would be drawn together by a heady aroma that came wafting from a point near the shack. The rich smell of food cooking over an open fire: Frances working her miracles over what must have been one of the original outdoor barbecues. The contrivance had been built up with stones to support an iron grill acquired from a secondhand dealer who had scrounged it from a street drain. Florence, in her role as assistant, would have earlier taken a big hubbard squash and broken it into pieces with an axe. Frances prepared these pieces with great care, and placed them in the improvised oven. The mouthwatering results became legendary. "When Frances cooked squash it was like nobody else's," explained a one-time regular. When financially possible, a typical menu featured thick steaks cooked over the grill, squash and fresh fruit.

Delilah's contribution to these idyllic outings was to sit on the back stoop and bark incessantly throughout the entire week-end. Everyone but the Girls could have cheerfully poisoned her.

The farm itself remained a wild tangle of growth. The land was basically poor, and after the wonderful early gardens, it produced only a little asparagus, a few wild quince, and a lot of poison ivy, which Florence rooted out with great energy and burned—leaves, stems, roots and all. Those who knew her well laughingly pronounced this as symbolic of Florence—the rooting out of evil.

Once darkness closed in around the cabin on summer evenings, visitors who happened to be there spent a great deal of time rescuing moths that had become trapped inside the lighted screened porch. This was another of Florence's pet works. A tumbler was placed over each moth that came to rest on the screen, a piece of paper slapped over the mouth of the glass, and the creature carried to the door and carefully released into the night.

While these good works were being performed, Frances would entertain at length with fascinating gossip and salacious tales. But, as Keith pointed out, "The trouble with Frances' tales is they enlarge so at each telling that it's impossible to remember the original story."

There was one tale that needed no elaboration.

It was a very hot Sunday afternoon. A group from the farm had gathered at the Rouge Valley Inn and were sitting enjoying a few cold beers on the terrace which overlooked a pond. Many people were in swimming. After a time one of the Girls' group, a young reporter with the *Star*, decided to join the swimmers. It seemed a wise idea, as he had definitely had more than just a few social beers, and a dunking could do nothing but good. He had earlier borrowed one of the ancient bathing suits kept at the shack for guests, so into the water he went, swimming leisurely out toward the diving platform. He climbed up onto the tower, he dove in, circled back, and climbed up for another dive, quite unaware he had left his suit in the water. There were audible gasps from the terrace, which was largely patronized by farmers with their wives and daughters on a Sunday outing. The Loring-Wyle group was in hysterics. Three or four men of their party finally regained sufficient presence of mind to surround their friend and do a disappearing act with him. While life may not have been easy for Florence and Frances, at least it was never dull.

"Even with a tree, you have to study its anatomy. If you ever want to teach anybody to paint a tree, or draw a tree, have him go inside and see there's an anatomy involved."

It was the essential code for the Girls. "A knowledge of anatomy gives vitality, vigour to sculpture."

Although for a long time neither of them took change seriously, they were distressed when change began to burrow under the foundations of classic tradition. "They dare to flout things nature does so well," grieved Florence.

How could they think otherwise? Both had extensive training based on five or six millennia of artistic tradition which evolved around the representation of the human figure. Anatomy had been the core of sculpture since Grecian times. But by 1925 the sculptor Brancusi, working in Paris, had already made his thrilling "Bird in Space," which was a complete departure from the norm. By using only the sparest of lines and extreme simplification of form, he had managed to catch the ecstatic, joyous freedom of a bird in flight—and without regard for its precise anatomy. It was a long while before the Girls could accept the truth of such work, and they could never have followed a parallel path.

"No good work is old-fashioned," protested Florence, not defensively, but because she knew it to be true. And so, with a dedication that was in itself a thing of beauty, the Girls pursued their convictions until the end of their lives. Their best work stands as their justification, while their lesser pieces expose the weariness of old concepts.

Frances could produce a classically perfect figure, a figure that could not be faulted technically—but so absolutely dull that it would summon only a ripple of surface interest. Yet, out of roughly the same period could come her wonderful portrait of Frederick Banting, a portrait that has been classed among the finest ever sculpted in this country. It is a splendid likeness and technically excellent, but more important, she has caught in it the questing, pioneer spirit of the man himself. Strength and character thrust out through the bronze, with the rugged simplicity of the brilliant doctor accented in the surface modelling treatment. The bust is alive and will never be old-fashioned.

Florence's sculpture was more even in quality. Her "Study of a Young Girl," shown at the Royal Academy in the early thirties, was an outstanding embodiment of her lyric reaction to clay and modelling. Its forms flow into one another with an easy grace that suggests the ephemeral purity of idealistic youth. Unlike her less successful pieces in which a striving for perfection of form sometimes stifled the life of the figure, restrained vigour pulses through the young girl, giving womanliness and fibre to her charm. The work was never sold.

Florence also excelled at relief portraits. She considered them quick studies but they were very perceptive interpretations of character. The portrait of old Mr. Loring is not only finely crafted, but vibrant with the flint of the old gentleman. Her specialty, though, was children. Her portraits of youngsters were full of her wonder for young creatures, human, furred or feathered—their feckless gaiety, their shining innocence, their touching vulnerability. She often worked children into her fountain figures.

If she felt the need of a model she might requisition visitors, and many who came to visit stayed to pose, as did the baby daughter of Charles and Louise Comfort. A fountain in need of a baby figure was underway, and little Ruth was held in position on her mother's knee, a blanket loosely draped ready to ward against the endemic cold of the studio. Louise Comfort herself once posed for Florence who was doing a kneeling figure and needed the soles of someone's feet for reference.

One rather unusual interpretation of her recurrent mother-and-child theme was the composition called "Chicago." Perhaps she had made a nostalgic pilgrimage back to the city that had been her home during the formative period of her career, and was struck by the phenomenal growth that had taken place. Whatever the inspiration, she conceived a design to express her feelings about the new Chicago. Using massive form, she presented the city as a solid, well-rooted parent figure, supporting at her knees an energetic boy-child restive with growth.

Frances sculpted by fits and starts. She was a very intense and rapid worker, so that she was either sculpting, body, heart and soul, or not at all. It suited her impulsive nature and allowed her to fit her other impulses, like politics, into the scheme of things.

Her brother's eldest son Bill once witnessed an almost miraculous example of her intense drive. He was, at the time, spending a year at the Church while he attended Northern Vocational School. He went to bed one evening on his cot in the studio, drowsily watching his aunt moulding clay onto the framework of what was to be a large turkey. It was far from recognizable. When he awoke in the morning he was confronted by a magnificent bird—an over-life-size turkey cock in full regalia. Frances had worked all night.

There was, in fact, a tremendous output of work from the Church in the thirties, but after Florence's "Torso" most of it was on speculation. They even did portraits of acquaintances who were unable to purchase. Finally their old friend, architect John Pearson, came up with commissions for each of them to develop fountain figures for R. S. McLaughlin's garden in Oshawa.

They also did a bit of teaching, which had its own frustrations. Florence wrote to H. O. McCurry, who had succeeded as Director of the National Gallery after Eric Brown's untimely death, "Great Scott! I am weary—two unruly, nice, self-willed pampered young ladies studying sculpture with me every morning." She also filled in as instructor for the sculpture class at Central Technical School when Elizabeth Hahn took leave of absence to give birth to a daughter. Both of the Girls took any form of teaching very seriously —as a sort of sacred mission to pass things along to the next generation.

Friendship with Frederick Banting was a source of mutual respect and enjoyment. He attended the salon of the early- and mid-thirties regularly, and usually came along to the Saturday-night parties. Not ordinarily a loquacious man, he knew the poems of Robert Service by heart and on occasion recited them at great length to the company. Often when sitting downstairs having supper late at night, he would make quick pen or pencil sketches of the faces around the table. At times he would have to leave around midnight, to go home "to feed the chickens," a duty related to some experimental work in his lab. Three a.m. would find him back at the Church to rejoin the still effervescent party.

As the group sat there around the table, their features highlighted under the glow of light from the lamp overhead, Frances could not help but respond to the powerful bone structure of Banting's face and the quiet assertion of his personality. Predictably, she persuaded him to sit for a portrait, and the experience of the sittings forged a deep and unbreakable bond. As she once explained, "Anyone you have sculpted belongs to you in a sense after that. Part of them belongs to you always."

Florence encountered this same phenomenon when she modelled the portrait of John Goss. Both Girls were fond of Goss. It was a great event when he came to town on a concert tour—"John Goss and the London Singers." On one such occasion, Florence managed to corner him long enough to make a full study of his head in clay. Oddly enough, although their bond of affection was reinforced, friends thought her portrait of him lacked the vitality of their bond. Their opinion emphasizes the general consensus that Florence's portraits of her friends were not her best work. Perhaps she hesitated to strip them of their shell, to bare their inner traits to the scrutiny of the world.

If distinguished company and creative work made up the warp of life in the Church, it must be observed animals made up the woof. Anyone spending the night might expect to share a couch with two or three cats. One student, opening a drawer to look for some equipment, nearly expired from heart failure on finding Beautiful, an immense black Persian with topaz eyes, coiled inside. During tough times friends suspected that the cats were cornering the lion's share of the food in the establishment. One cat refused to eat anything except tinned salmon, which had to be set out on a particular tile on the dining room floor. "Why not?" Florence defended. "Why shouldn't a cat have its own preferences? We do. It has every right to its own preferences."

For the uninitiated, it was quite unnerving to visit the Church at night. Cats materialized eerily out of the shadows. Perched on stands. Peered around sculptures. Stretched atop bookcases.

Sometimes a group of visitors would arrive together at the door. "Well now, why don't you all sit down" would be the unfailing greeting. The bunch would eye one another knowingly and laugh. "Oh!" Florence would exclaim. "Of course." And she would move around dumping out all the cats that were curled like big muffs in the amazing collection of dilapidated armchairs. It was necessary to sit down quickly, though, or the cats would reclaim their territory.

Delilah was never required to vacate her spot in the only really comfortable chair—near the fire. The only challenge to this mangy princess came from a rat, newly returned after the years of banishment. It would march up to Delilah with cool confidence, confiscate any bone from under the nose of the mesmerized animal, and scurry down the stairs with it. When Delilah grew so old that she could no longer walk, the Girls would carry her outside in a blanket sling to lie in the sun. Finally there were excited phone calls: "Did you hear the good news? Delilah's dead!"

In the mid-thirties, almost as a desperate act of faith, Frances conceived the "Goal Keeper." Times were so difficult that she had to risk a large work on speculation; she could not sit on her hands and despair. Hockey had become a major interest and even Frances found its young men, with their high-powered skills, very exciting. She envisaged an immense goalie to epitomize the thrilling sport. Some obscure authority apparently encouraged her to undertake the task, with the implicit understanding that Maple Leaf Gardens was unofficially interested in such a figure.

That was all the encouragement she needed. She started in to build a figure that was to be seven feet tall—heroic to suit the subject. The Gardens agreed to lend her hockey pads and equipment as models for the project, and when her nephew Frank came from school at week-ends she had him don the uniform and pose. In time everyone

op left: Florence Wyle, 1886

*op right: The Wyle twins, Florence
nd Frank*

*ottom left: Frances Loring, Spokane,
Vash., 1897*

ottom right: Frances Loring, 1890

Above: Frances Loring, near Cobalt, Ontario, 1908

Top right: Frances Loring, New York, 1911

Bottom right: Portrait of Wyle by Loring (plaster), c. 1911. Bequeathed to The National Gallery of Canada, Ottawa

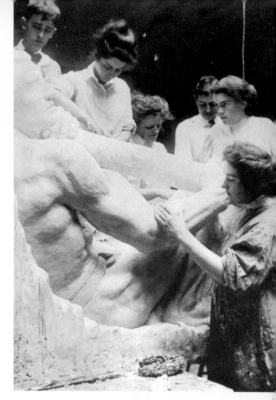

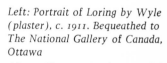

Left: Portrait of Loring by Wyle (plaster), c. 1911. Bequeathed to The National Gallery of Canada, Ottawa

Above: Florence Wyle, second from left, at the Chicago Art Institute

Loring-Wyle studio, MacDougal Alley, New York, c. 1911-1913

Above: Frances Loring, Florence Wyle, Church Street, Toronto, 1914

Opposite page at top: A meeting of the selection committee for the Canadian section of the British Empire Exhibition in Wembley, England, 1924. From left: Clarence Gagnon, RCA; Florence Wyle, ARCA, OSA, SSC; Frederick Challoner, RCA, OSA; Randolph Hewton; Horatio Walker; Eric Browne, Director, The National Gallery; E. Wyley Grier, PRCA, OSA; Harry McCurry, Secretary; Franklin Brownell, RCA; Arthur Lismer, ARCA, OSA

*Above: Portrait of Frederick Varley
(plaster), by Florence Wyle, c. 1922.
Bronze edition purchased 1956, The
National Gallery of Canada, Ottawa*

*Right: Portrait of A. Y. Jackson
(plaster), by Florence Wyle, c. 1943.
Bronze edition purchased 1956, The
National Gallery of Canada, Ottawa*

Right: Torso (plaster), by Florence Wyle,
c. 1930. Marble edition purchased 1933,
The National Gallery of Canada, Ottawa

Below: Study of a Girl (plaster), by Florence
Wyle, c. 1931. In the Loring-Wyle Estate

Centre: Chicago (plaster), by Florence Wyle,
c. 1933

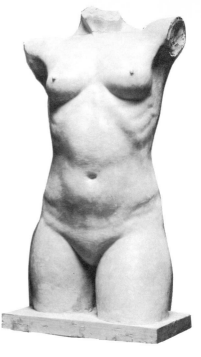

Left: Girl Rod Turner (bronze), by Frances Loring, 1918. Canadian War Records Collection, The National Gallery of Canada, Ottawa

Below: War Memorial, St. Stephen, N.B. (clay model), by Frances Loring, 1919

Left: *The Church as it was until 1952*
Above: *The Church, 1958*
Below left: *The Girls having tea, 1952*
Below: *The Girls at work in the Church, 1952*

Above: Sir Robert Borden, by Frances Loring—clay models, from maquette to full-sized portrait head, 1953-1957. The full-size bronze edition is on Parliament Hill.

Opposite page above: Lion, Queen Elizabeth Way (stone), by Frances Loring, 1940.

Opposite page below: Frances Loring, 1963, with portrait of Sir Frederick Banting (plaster), c. 1935, bronze editions 1950 and 1966. The bust was presented to the Academy of Medicine, Toronto, by Lady Henrietta Banting through the courtesy of the Ely Lilly Company of Indianapolis.

THE QUEEN ELIZABETH WAY WAS OPENED BY THE KING AND QUEEN IN JUNE 1939
KING THE FIRST VISIT OF A REIGNING SOVEREIGN TO A SISTER DOMINION OF THE EMPI
COURAGE AND RESOLUTION OF THEIR MAJESTIES IN UNDERTAKING THE ROYAL VISIT
OF IMMINENT WAR HAVE INSPIRED THE PEOPLE OF THIS PROVINCE TO COMPLETE TI
K IN THE EMPIRES DARKEST HOUR IN FULL CONFIDENCE OF VICTORY AND A LASTING PEA

Interior of studio, 1958

Florence at work in the new wing, 1962

Florence Wyle, with Young Mother (bronze), c. 1928

—nephews, students, friends—were conscripted to haul clay and slap it onto the towering armature. Florence began to murmur protestingly over the amount of clay the mammoth was devouring. Over a ton of it was needed before the bulky pads were completely roughed in. But Frances, fired by enthusiasm, carried blithely on. A young neighbour, content to be paid in fruit and cookies, came in after school during the week to put on the equipment and stand as a model. It took two years to develop the work from maquette through to finished plaster cast.

Despite the problems of producing such a large figure with limited resources, Frances somehow managed to carry it out—a gigantic feat in the frigid temperature of the studio. It was fantastically difficult to keep the damp clay figure from freezing. Even the gas line into the Church froze in severe weather. It was the Girls' usual practice to sculpt small figures in winter so they could be trundled close to the stove. The Goalie, now an enormous, heavy bulk of damp clay, defied manoeuvring. But somehow Frances kept it from freezing.

Finally the day came when the giant was to be cast in plaster. He was to have his trial run in the forthcoming Sculptors' Society show. Florence happened to be casting two heads for the same exhibit, and the event of the casting provides a clear illustration of the contrast between their working habits.

Keith and another young Scotsman, Ian Cameron, were on hand for the monumental task. The two fellows flung themselves into the job, dashing down from the studio to the bathroom in the basement —the only source of running water—and rushing back to the scene of action with fresh pails of plaster. Total involvement. Frances, teetering on a ladder, slopped wet plaster onto the clay figure with great force. She did nothing gently. Plaster was everywhere.

Across the room, in a small area of calm, an oasis in the hectic shambles of the studio, Florence sat quietly reading a book. A newspaper lay neatly on the floor to her right, and on it reposed the two heads, waiting while the plaster set. On another newspaper to her left lay her tools, chisel and hammer at the ready.

Florence's casts were always a marvel in precision, as thin as possible, yet still functional, while Frances' cast were thick, solid,

57

substantial, and required extra work when being chipped away.

Sadly, after the tremendous effort that had gone into his creation, the "Goal Keeper" was not a great artistic success. He was certainly impressive, admirable, but he did not quite convey the feeling of superbly conditioned youth, or the tense drive underlying the skilled discipline of a goalie, qualities that would have given the work lasting validity. Frances was fond of him, however. This was one of the very few instances in her career when her enthusiasm out-weighed her realistic appraisal.

The Goalie was shown a number of times. Their cartage man and good friend John Murphy could vouch for that, as it was his job to transport the massive plaster on each occasion.

And the figure did have its advocates. After the S.S.C. exhibition Frances was encouraged by the same obscure source to set the "Goal Keeper" up in the Maple Leaf Gardens on her own initiative. How, then, could the authorities resist it? She did so. Reaction fol-lowed quickly. A telephone call from the President of the Gardens: "Get that thing out of here. It's taking up too much room!" The Goalie was ignominiously retired.

Though the giant was something of a white elephant, "Eskimo Woman and Child" was not. Frances' initial inspiration derived from a photograph of an Eskimo mother carrying her baby on her back. It had been taken in the Arctic by anthropologist Dr. Diamond Jenness.

First she developed a model about three feet high. Then, un-willing to lose the interesting detail of clothes in the overall design, she went on to develop it into a life-size figure. The finished work was much admired when shown, but as feared, no prospects of sale materialized. It was not until twenty-five years later that it was sold—to the National Gallery. "Not the usual ending of a work done on spec," Frances commented wryly.

Another vital work was her "Miner," a head which was inspired by the Moose River mining disaster in 1936. The miners were trapped in the mine cave-in for five days before they were finally rescued. Because of her mining background, the drama was bound to have tremendous impact on Frances, and her "Miner" was a tribute to the courage and stamina required of mining men.

Throughout the Depression the Girls continued to maintain a happy relationship with their oldest and more immediate neighbours. They saw one another over many a difficult hurdle with mutual kindness. But as the years pushed along, life altered on Glenrose Avenue. The Church no longer sat on orchard land with only a handful of houses. The city had crept insidiously in their direction until it engulfed them completely. The informality of the country lane gave way to the self-conscious respectability of a city street. The church at number 110 became a source of exasperation to some of the newer residents, who referred to it as "that dreadful eyesore!" From the point of view of tax-paying, community-proud citizens, these objections held a certain element of validity. The Girls were by now well into middle age, and with a heavy work load and no money, were having some difficulty keeping the building in repair. They tried to keep the grass cut, but it was next to impossible to mow neatly around the woodpiles. Many of their new neighbours, to their own great loss, never knew or cared that the two eccentric women in the studio were famous people whose quality was known across the country.

The children knew, though. The Church and its owners were of endless fascination to them. The Clay Ladies, the youngsters titled them. Visits to the studio were highlights in the lives of successive generations of local children.

"Can we see the Hockey Player?" they asked. Or, if they had seen him many times before, "Our cousin would like to see the Hockey Player." They could all identify with him and he was often their excuse to get in to see the other mysteries of the place.

The Girls valued these visitors highly and experienced few disciplinary problems with even the most boisterous among them. Usually each child was given a lump of clay out of the tub to take home. Florence always talked to them as though they were adults and perfectly equal. Although her little discourses must have been obscure, the children would listen avidly as she explained the intricacies of design or showed them how to draw a bird. "Nobody sees things any more! A bird's legs don't go straight down from its body." The visits were not complete without an admonition to be kind to animals.

It was a curious situation. Although the Girls must have presented a most unusual picture to the neighbourhood as they walked Delilah up the street of an evening—scarves flowing, trousers bagging, Frances keeping Delilah in line with her cane—they were never objects of derision to the children. Cruel and thoughtless though the young can be to people who function outside the familiar, they never poked fun at these two, never treated them as eccentrics. The attractively eerie atmosphere around the Church at night, with the dim lighting showing through the pointed windows, should have made it a natural target for pranks. But it was not. Instinctively the children brushed aside the surface idiosyncrasies to recognize what was hidden to many of the adults—the very tangible worth of the Clay Ladies and the interesting work that went on in the Church.

Among their peers, their appearance was not considered out of the way at all. Sculptor Elford Cox recalls meeting them for the first time at a picnic in the summer of 1937, and remembers them as fine-looking, alert and intelligent. Yet it would be misleading to suggest that they were ordinary-looking people. Picture them perhaps at an exhibition opening at the Art Gallery of Toronto. No one could miss them. Frances loved to make an entrance in some stunning costume, and is known to have appeared in purple velvet with gold fringe. She edged closer and closer to the obese as the years passed, but she wore her weight like a Hawaiian queen. "Here comes the ice-breaker," someone once remarked without malice or ridicule as she was noticed forging her way through a dense crowd of open-nighters. The sea of people simply parted as she advanced. Her costume was never complete without a stream of cigarette ash adorning her ample bosom. She was a chain smoker, and it was disconcerting to anyone with whom she was talking to watch helplessly as her ash grew longer and longer, curving relentlessly downward from her cigarette until it finally, inevitably, plopped, unnoticed by her, to join the pile below.

Florence would have been disconcerted had she realized that she, too, made an impact by the visual effect of her appearance and the verbal effect of her wit. Her ensemble was not calculated to catch the eye, but did in spite of itself. Who could dismiss the long, makeshift skirt that looked suspiciously as though it had once been a velvet curtain? Or the man's white shirt sporting an incongruous bit of scraggly velvet ribbon tied in a bow beneath the collar? Or the heavy Oxfords poking out below the skirt? She would move about, making fitful progress through the crowd, warmly greeted as she went by those she knew. Although large gatherings had the effect of dazing her, she could always snap to alertness long enough to prick the odd pretentious balloon if the hot air was more than she could tolerate, or to pass a few biting comments on any work she considered not up to par. Equally, she was never chary with praise. On the whole, however, sophisticated gatherings were not her natural environment.

Back in the Church, parties were still the oiling ingredient that kept the work cycle from turning too tightly on itself. The most delightful times were the Christmas get-togethers. There would be a chosen few for dinner, with a larger group of forty or fifty people invited for the evening. Keith was always on hand to assist in the extensive preparations, and he customarily cooked the turkey. He had made another great plank table and this was pulled up to the earlier one to form a great T. Both groaned under the weight of the steaming food. By the time the company had assembled, a fire would be blazing in the hearth, flickering long fingers of light and shadow against the mellow brick walls of the basement room. The tables would be suffused by the warm glow from candles stuck in wine bottles. No one thought to take exception to the chipped crockery, or the questionable cleanliness of the place, or the cats on the table. Afterwards there would be Christmas music in the studio upstairs.

One year, when living was particularly precarious, Frances and Florence decided that if there was any money for Christmas, it should be spent on children. They felt there must be children who needed things, but whose parents would never ask for help. Accordingly, the Girls and their friends found a number of such needy families and arranged to pick them up on the day of the party. There were about forty mothers and children all together. Half a dozen turkeys were cooked. Santa Claus arrived. But it was very hard to get the children to warm up. Nobody wanted to speak to anyone else. Some of the mothers had reservations about a few of their fellow guests. "I don't think you ought to have Mrs. So-and-So here. She gets *Star* Fund relief."

There were presents for everyone—sweaters and warm clothing —things that were needed, but not exactly things the children wanted. One family who lived just down the street and who had arrived on foot, insisted on being driven home like the others, because they had never been in a car.

"We never did it again," said Frances. "I felt like Ruth Draper in the 'Garden Party.' I felt as though I were patronizing them." But they continued to provide Christmas for artists, many of them almost destitute, which was perhaps fulfilling as needy a function.

The late thirties found the Girls still struggling. They took on the job of producing a series of figures for the National Museum in Ottawa. These were studies of the native peoples of Canada as they would have been in their original state, before the coming of the white man. It was less than exciting work for creative artists, but it meant food on the table.

The autumn of 1938 was a gratifying period for Florence. She was elected to the rank of full Academician in the Royal Canadian Academy, the fourth woman—and the first woman sculptor—to be elected since the society's inception in 1880. (Marion Long and Lilias Newton, both painters, had been similarly honoured just prior to this, and Charlotte Schreiber had been elected soon after the founding of the R.C.A.)

The following year Frances became involved in a series of radio broadcasts on "Great Sculpture," sponsored by the National Gallery. She was a natural for this sort of challenge. With her calm self-assurance and a wonderful command of words, she could express herself succinctly and with the added dash of spirit that made for exciting listening. But she never cared for her own voice on radio. She dropped her inflection at the end of certain sentences and the resulting accentuation came through as vaguely pompous, which annoyed her.

At last, in 1938, prospects began to look a little brighter for the Girls. Architect William Sommerville commissioned them to create a number of bird panels for the Harry Oakes Pavilion at Niagara Falls.

Before they were finished, Sommerville arrived breathless at the studio one day to outline a further project for a coat of arms for the new customs building at Niagara. "When do you want it?" they asked. "We wanted it yesterday!" he answered. So the two of them went at it together. The plaque was the only joint effort of their long careers. As a coat of arms is so stylized in design, there was no danger of interfering with one another's interpretations, or of stepping on one another's convictions.

Once again friends were able to sigh with relief. "Thank God, Florence and Frances will have enough to make things a bit easier for a while!" They might have known better. With a substantial part of her share from these ventures, and with Florence's full approbation, Frances had her "Dream Within a Dream" carved in marble from the original plaster she had modelled back in New York days. She too was a gambler.

CHAPTER

6

Despite the anxiety that overshadowed and invaded all normal activity, the early war years were, surprisingly, ones of relative prosperity for the Girls.

The surge of luck on which they had been riding continued. A job came for Florence. She was asked to create a monument in memory of Edith Cavell, the World War I nurse who had been shot by the Germans in Belgium for her work in aiding the escape of over two hundred wounded British, French and Belgian soldiers.

Florence designed a large bronze bas-relief which depicted Edith Cavell supporting two wounded soldiers. All lines in the composition were delineated to contribute to a mood of deep compassion. It was a definitive piece of work, beautifully modelled with the rhythmic yet precise discipline that marks outstanding relief sculpture.

The finished bronze panel was erected on the grounds of the Toronto General Hospital at the corner of University Avenue and College Street. An inscription in bronze was part of the over-all design.

Then one day, without a word from anyone, official or otherwise, a bronze wreath appeared, fastened permanently to the stone below the relief. "If I'd intended it I'd have done it myself when I made the thing!" Florence commented crisply. The gratuitous decoration had been added to the panel by a certain ethnic group who thought to contribute to the war effort by installing these wreaths at a number of strategic sites. Under the circumstances no authorities wished to interfere, let alone remove the wreath from the Cavell monument. It would have been a somewhat doubtful task in any case due to the wonderfully efficient manner in which the offending piece had been permanently bolted to the stone.

There was little alternative but to accept the situation as gracefully as possible.

Continuing a pattern of almost unbelievable regularity, the next commission followed right after that of the relief. This time it was Frances' turn. She was to create a lion to sit at the base of a column at the Toronto entrance to the Queen Elizabeth Highway. The monument was being erected to commemorate the 1939 visit of King George VI and Queen Elizabeth. On June 7th of that year Queen Elizabeth had officially opened the newly completed super-highway running from Toronto to Niagara Falls. Frances Loring was chosen as the sculptor whose work, with its monumental qualities, was most suited to the project in mind. It was the most prestigious commission she had received up to that time.

"Why a lion?" someone asked Frances.

"A British Lion, sir!" she pointed out. "A snarling, defiant British Lion, eight feet high," she specified further in a letter to Harry McCurry.

Florence was involved as well, but only to a modest degree. She modelled a relief portrait of the Queen and her husband, to be incorporated on the column which was to rise behind the lion.

Initially Frances developed several maquettes. A half-size model was built up in clay from the chosen design. From the resulting half-size plaster cast, the work was enlarged and cut in stone. The interpretation itself was highly stylized, which was a considerable feat in this case. Hundreds of sculptors from the time of the Egyptians and Assyrians had tried their hand at stylizing the lion, leaving little to be said in monumental form about that regal beast.

Frances was aware of the inherent pitfalls of attempting to be original within the confines of an overworn motif. As might be imagined, she had the strength of conviction to completely discard preconceived ideas of the lion in sculpture. She started instead with the beast in its natural state and she translated this into a tangible symbol of England's position at the beginning of the war. "Rising from a reclining position to fight," she explained. She infused a balance of tension that could be sensed running from the powerful paws to the end of the tail. "It's a thing that nature gives to an animal before he goes into fighting—a knowledge of the dramatic effect of that kind of pose."

Frances' projects seemed to become complicated beyond reasonable belief, almost as though to prove Murphy's Law: if something can go wrong it will. This undertaking lived up to the law; it was plagued with frustrations from beginning to end. In the first place, word was passed that Queenston limestone was to be the material used—as a patriotic gesture. Now limestone from the quarries in Queenston, admirable though it was for building purposes, was far from ideal for sculpture. It was very hard and characterized by little holes and pockets which marred the surface, a combination that made it difficult to carve. Indiana limestone would have been more suitable, and flawless stone was easily available in any size required. "We certainly objected to being patriotic as far as Queenston limestone goes," was the Girls' wry comment some years later.

The question of a stone carver was more serious—even alarming. Again, patriotism was the issue. A well-qualified Italian was found, but Frances was not allowed to hire him as he was considered an "enemy alien." Next came a German, reared and educated in Canada, but of course he was out too. Another Italian, Louis Temporale, got past the authorities but came up against fellow members of the stone-cutters union who pointed out that he, too, although he had lived in Canada since childhood, was unacceptable when it came to a government job. In desperation, Frances was forced to make do with an Englishman with whom she had worked uneasily on a previous job; she would never have hired him from choice. He very much resented working for and taking instructions from a woman, no matter how qualified she might be.

To top the situation off, he announced that he did not own a pointing machine, and had no idea where he could lay his hands on one. Without a pointing machine to register depths and measurements from the sculpted model for duplication or enlargement in another material, not even the most skilful carver could attempt to carve the Lion. But there seemed no such machines available in the country and, because of the war, no possibility of importing one. Frantic inquiries by Frances finally brought rumour of one that had been used by Walter Allward during the carving of the memorial at

Vimy Ridge. Evidently it had been mouldering ever since in a store-room belonging to the Engineers' Branch of the Department of National Defence. It was unearthed and made available for the carving of the Lion.

At last all was apparently under control. Frances resigned herself to her less-than-satisfactory carver, trusting to the vitality and strength of the design to assert itself over indifference.

The Lion had to be carved on the site, as the stone from which he was to emerge jutted out as an extension from the base of the limestone column—part of the architectural concept designed by W. L. Sommerville. Since the actual cutting in stone did not get underway until August, there was going to be a race against winter.

Frances kept a supervisory eye on the carving of her beast. Progress was slow. Pressure mounted. It was while making a routine check at the site that Frances, who had been trying her best to keep relations with her carver on a workable plane, was burdened with that final straw that broke the camel's back. "I've changed the line a little on the neck, Miss Loring. I thought it would look a bit better."

She fired him on the spot.

Her satisfaction was short-lived. The Lion was still a month away from completion, and as she well knew, there was not another cutter in the country who was both competent to carve sculpture and at the same time "nationally" acceptable to the authorities. With that genius for impelling action that was peculiarly hers, she came to a spontaneous decision. Fie on union rules that restricted professional carving to union ranks! She would finish the Lion herself. The union did not dare to stand in the way of her determination.

The odds were much against her. The only piece of stone carving she had ever attempted had been a mother and child composition back in the New York days—nearly thirty years earlier. Certainly she had never handled the power tools necessary in this large undertaking. And it was now November and late autumn winds were howling in off Lake Ontario.

She threw all her energies into reducing the odds of nature and inexperience. With a protective tarpaulin erected around her, she attacked the power tools and wielded them to her purpose. She completed her Lion with as polished a skill as any professional stone cutter.

Unfortunately, she paid dearly for the experience in terms of personal suffering. From this point on, the arthritis that had been nagging of late, moved in with an agonizing grip to plague her for the rest of her days.

But she considered the result worth the price. The Lion was magnificent. It has often been cited as the finest piece of architectural sculpture in the country. It represents not only the defiance of a beleaguered nation, but the indomitable courage of a lone woman.

Oddly enough, the comments at the time of unveiling did not rise to the achievement. The artist had to be satisfied with simply knowing within herself that she had fulfilled a deep commitment. "We were too busy winning the war to make comments on sculpture. Nobody was interested much in anything like that." Frances accepted the situation with equanimity.

Commissions continued to come in with welcome regularity. In 1941, the designs that had been submitted some time earlier for decorations to be used on the approach to the new Rainbow Bridge at Niagara, were at last authorized. It was a somewhat ambiguous situation for sculptors. As Frances wrote to a colleague, "Government is so scared . . . that the Opposition should realize that art is being indulged in during wartime, that the work is being sort of sneaked in as construction work." The job included some lovely floral emblems by Florence, and reliefs of stylized northern landscapes. Frances took on the portrayal of industrial progress in the province, and followed that with a large deer panel for the Niagara Parks Commission.

When these works were completed, the Girls' run of luck suddenly broke. Nothing more came their way until after the war ended. There were no commissions. Nothing was sold. It was the most difficult period of their long careers. Yet, as Frances put it, "I don't think we were ever hungry." And she laughed. "Probably better if I had been." She recalled that the worst of the food problem was the boredom, the monotony of the fare they could afford.

They might have eaten better except that, true to their long-established custom of investing in major improvements while there was a bit of cash on hand, they had arranged to install a furnace in the Church—a giant octopus of a creature with arms going up every which-way—in an attempt to spread heat into the farthest corners of the Church. Its awkward hulk brooding there in the room behind the kitchen did not fire one with conviction in its competence. However, its appearance belied its great heating power, which revolutionized the life in the Church. No longer did a meeting in the studio of one of the art societies feature the gradual convergence of all chairs on the stove until, by the time the meeting was adjourned, as many members as possible had their feet up on the iron guard-rail. No longer did an invitation to supper in winter include the admonition to "wear something warm." And the heat was kind to joints creaking with arthritis.

The parties continued, but they were not so lively nor so frequent. Now and then there would be a special occasion. When A. Y. Jackson came down from the North with a fresh batch of sketches, the Girls usually held a "sketch party," which was actually a showing of his new oil studies. Food was not a great problem then. Most guests, when invited, knew enough to ask, "What can I bring?"

Happily, despite the gloom of war and the lack of commissions, Frances and Florence never lost their sense of fun nor their enjoyment of the ridiculous. From time to time, when the going was particularly difficult, they would declare that they were contemplating suicide. But then, they reasoned, their demise would not be of great value unless they took along a few others with them. They then would proceed to draw up a list of a dozen people the world would be well rid of. MacKenzie King always headed the list.

Money was very scarce. A close friend, Jean Irving, who spent a great deal of time with them, remembered the laundryman coming along one day and apologetically presenting a long overdue bill.

"Certainly," said Frances, and wrote him a cheque.

As soon as he left they rushed down to their bank to transfer enough funds from their "last-ditch" account to cover the cheque. "He needs it worse than we do," they murmured.

The secret of their survival was undoubtedly the fact that they lived simply. Both were quite capable of stringent austerity. Frances had been brought up to adjust to feast or famine and was eminently qualified for living up to one and down to the other. Florence was a product of strict puritan simplicity, and probably never found it difficult to deny herself comforts, although she would have suffered terribly if the animals could not have been decently fed. They both cherished being able to give work to some starving young sculptor, even if it was only to haul out an old plaster unobtrusively and pretend that they badly needed it recast.

Even in the best times, they had never allowed themselves to become dependent on an extravagant standard of living. Once when a large cheque had been cashed, Frances was tempted to light her cigarette with a five dollar bill, but stopped herself.

"Think how many people that would feed in a day in starving India!"

Early in the forties, the Federation of Canadian Artists was formed. Frances and Florence attended the Kingston conference which laid out its framework. The new organization was to be an alliance of artists and those in related professions, to promote the arts in Canada.

Florence had never been much of a believer in meetings. "A waste of time!" she dismissed them once. But of the F.C.A. she was more hopeful. She thought that it might very well promote a more communal spirit in art.

Frances was very optimistic about the possibilities of the federation, and welcomed it as an implementation of her own hopes for concerted action by artists for themselves. She brought an interesting suggestion before the Kingston conference with regard to the role of artists in wartime: steps should be taken "to counteract the feeling, which is rather general, that it is a disgrace to in any way patronize art until the war is over." She insisted that the artist had a valid contribution to make toward the success of the war effort and toward life in the community, and should not be treated as a type of irresponsible parasite. More than this, she felt that artists themselves needed to know that their art was a positive contribution in time of trouble.

Not satisfied merely to state her case, she gave it practical credence by showing how sculpture could be put to work. Most men, she pointed out, enjoyed whittling and carving. Why not use this as an approach to sculpture, to give soldiers in camps an interest that might be of great help to them in times of enforced illness? Little equipment was needed, and a few lessons would enable them to carry on by themselves. Competitions between groups would add stimulation.

In fact, her novel idea attracted genuine interest from the Department of National Defence, and resulted in a booklet, *Woodcarving for Pleasure*, which Frances wrote. It was published by the Canadian Legion Educational Services in cooperation with the Y.M.C.A. War Services.

She also found herself doing a series of radio broadcasts on "What Artists are in the War." Her audience always included at least two avid listeners. Florence and Frances' nephew Tom (who was staying with them on vacation from school) would sit at home, ears glued to a borrowed radio. There was always some doubt as to the set's reliability and on at least one occasion it failed completely and they had to rush next door to listen with some neighbours.

Although Florence applauded Frances' performing talent, she could not have emulated her in that type of public projection. Not that she was mute on issues—anything but. She was a constant defender of the faith as it applied to artists, but preferred her confrontations face to face. Her small stature and gentle appearance were absolutely deceptive. Let anyone give her an ideal to defend and, as one friend said, "God help you!" Another friend once cut into one of her dissertations with an exasperated, "Florence, we love you in spite of your virtues!" Florence stopped immediately to laugh heartily at herself. At least she did not take herself too seriously.

The Girls differed drastically in their faith in group action. Frances personally saw a number of important issues settled successfully via the channels of various societies, but perhaps the thrust of her own conviction was instrumental in their success. On the other hand, Florence's scepticism over the motives and ultimate worth of group action was not unfounded. Her reaction to a meeting of the Federation of Canadian Artists held at the museum in Toronto was a case in point.

As usual, the meeting was dominated by several long-winded extroverts. The morning droned on with every indication that the garrulous participants would go on forever without moving any closer to decisive action. Finally an adjournment for lunch was announced, leaving all business suspended for further discussion in the afternoon. As the delegates prepared to rise and stretch their cramped muscles, a voice rang out from the back of the auditorium. "You people may be going out for lunch, but I'm going home!" Florence apparently felt she had heard it all too many times before.

Both Girls were in full accord, though, when it came to supporting the Sculptors' Society. The Church itself seemed to have become almost a national home for sculptors in the forties. Frances lobbied for them and for the society endlessly. When she was again elected president, after being absent from actual office for some years, she received a letter from H. O. McCurry. "Congratulations on your elevation to the presidency of the S.S.C. I had an impression all along that you were president anyway!"

While meetings were held at the studios of the various members, they most frequently took place in the Church. In the days before Florence's allergies, Frances would be puffing away like a smokestack, hammering out contract outlines and drafting letters of protest to this or that organization. Florence would sit there rolling cigarettes by hand and passing them over to Frances, who always had difficulty keeping them stuck together. Her direct participation was usually in the form of the odd incisive comment that set matters squarely in place. The gatherings tended to be incendiary affairs, with much squabbling back and forth between Frances (or Florence) and Emmanuel Hahn, and for variety, bursts of invective between Hahn and his wife, Elizabeth Wyn Wood, whose cool intellect could slice through trivia like a knife through wet clay. At times it was difficult for younger artists to survive in the crossfire.

One night Frances and Hahn had a terrible fight, which Frances won. Hahn got up in a towering rage, retrieved his coat, and stomped out to the door.

"Good-bye beloved!" Frances called gaily after him, with devilish glee.

Hahn turned, spat out, "God damn you to Hell!" and slammed the door resoundingly behind him.

Amazingly, the affairs of the society did move along. It was almost as though the principal contenders had agreed to disagree as long as it did not really disrupt business.

Occasionally it did affect others. When Dora de Pedery Hunt arrived as a refugee from Hungary, the Girls gave her immediate support and put her up for a membership in the society. But for several years she was turned down. She later found out that Hahn had voted against her. "Not that I think you're no good; I was opposed because Frances was voting for you!"

But the society was by no means run by the elder members alone. If some member were acting up, no matter how important a personage he was, the rest jumped on him. On one occasion, when Hahn was being particularly objectionable, he was told to either "shut up or leave!" The meeting was being held at his house.

In principle, neither Frances nor Florence allowed personal taste in art to influence their attitude toward younger sculptors. But when Elford Cox made his appearance as a sculptor after the war, with no training behind him and, worse, no wish for training, the Girls openly opposed his acceptance into the S.S.C. for three consecutive years. "The reason we kept you out was because you didn't know a bloody thing about anatomy," they later explained to him quite frankly.

Any other reaction was out of the question. To them, he and the new breed of young artists he represented were like illiterates pretending to be literary experts. How could they take their place among dedicated professionals? The Girls relented in Cox's case when they realized that he was serious in his purpose and had every intention of becoming as good a sculptor as possible, within his own definition. Perhaps they were never really able to forgive him his lack of training, but their about-face was unqualified. They met him on his own terms and extended to him the same undemanding helping hand that had gone out to so many others before.

Those were lively times for the society. After a meeting in the Church, they would all file downstairs for refreshments and talk around the big table, everybody straining to be heard above the din, everybody feeling for a brief hour that he was living in the art atmosphere of Paris at the beginning of the century.

Cox and Pauline Redsell, Alvin Hilts, Dora Hunt, Donald Stewart,

Cleeve and Jean Horne, Arthur Tracy, Stephen Trenka—all were there. So were Emmanuel and Elizabeth Hahn, hating the Girls, hating themselves, hating everybody and having a marvellous time. Florence freely dispensed judgments and made moral indictments which everyone accepted as absolute pronouncements. Frances kept a watchful eye on the needs of the guests. "More sausage, lamb?" Or she would cut across the hubbub to urge some salami on someone she thought was looking a bit thin.

When Donald Stewart became president of the society in 1947, the inaugural meeting was held out at the farm. It was just as well that the occasion was an outdoor picnic affair, because the farm was falling into absolute disrepair. The Girls, who were no longer able to make regular trips on week-ends, were saddened by the damage inflicted by vandals.

Stewart was around the studio a great deal in those years, often assisting with casting or other technical projects. Once he brought his two small sons to meet the Girls (who had almost become monuments in themselves), and to visit the Church, which had become something of a shrine to young sculptors. The boys didn't seem to be at all overawed by their surroundings, however. In fact, while their elders were occupied they busied themselves tearing up the S.S.C. ballots which were waiting to be tallied. Exit one very red-faced father and two chastened youngsters. When they had recovered from the shock, the Girls were very amused, and laughed about the episode for years.

It was a time when lighter moments were sorely needed. The later war years were a test of the steel that was in Florence Wyle and Frances Loring. Their survival seemed a miracle to anyone who was much around the Church. In spite of the stringency of their situation, there was always some young sculptor or other unfortunate hired to do odd jobs about the place—an arrangement that enabled the Girls to direct a little cash where it was desperately needed, without engendering any loss of self-respect.

And always there were the cats to be fed.

"Benjy," Florence was overheard to ask cat Benjamin Franklin, one Christmas night after Frances and a house-guest had at last retired, "will you have dark meat or light meat?"

The Girls were scandalized by the question of an undiscerning reporter who equated lack of income with lack of work. What hobbies filled their spare time?

"Spare time!" choked one from her work bench.

"Hobbies!" gasped the other from behind a mound of paper work.

The reporter beat an immediate retreat.

Once the war was over and it again became respectable for artists to be commissioned, several projects developed which provided both work and income. There was a considerable undertaking for the Bank of Montreal, some memorial tablets for schools, a figure for a fountain, and a madonna in marble for the Mothercraft Hospital in Toronto.

More frequent gala occasions, such as openings at the Art Gallery of Toronto, did reflect the post-war momentum that was affecting the art scene in general. In spite of advancing age, the Girls were still show-stoppers at such events. As one artist recalled, many of these rather conservative gatherings would not have been particularly memorable without the presence of the Girls. Frances was decked out in some sort of green satin cape, topped by a turban. She was splendid. Or, as one artist described her, "enough to terrify God." Florence, deaf to the call of fashion, had ceased making concessions to formal dress. For the next twenty years she found her ancient grey flannel suit quite adequate to any situation.

"They must be very wealthy," people concluded, when they caught sight of the pair of them in the crowd. Who else but wealthy eccentrics would dare to appear in such garb?

Then came 1948, and an unbelievable stroke of luck. Gravel had been discovered on the farm. Would they sell the rights? The old weed-choked, tumbledown farm. They let it go, regretfully, but retained the cabin on the hill for a minimal yearly sum. Eleven thousand dollars, and more followed. At last, after so many bitterly difficult times, the pressure of carrying on with never enough was relieved.

"Hurrah!" said Florence, whose garden behind the Church was evidently needing attention. "Now I can buy a load of manure."

It is not ugliness that kills
But lack of beauty—
If man's soul is not enraptured
Warmed and pulsed by beauty's fire
He dies—slowly, but as surely
As forgotten unsunned flowers
In winter die.

(From *Poems*, by Florence Wyle)

Florence was essentially a person of innate modesty. This is not to say that she suffered from a sense of inferiority, but that it was in her most basic nature to be retiring. No one, for instance, but her very intimate friends knew her to be a poet. She celebrated her love of nature and creation in her sculpture. But some things cannot be expressed in solid form; they need the ether of poetry.

Words came to her as she walked in the fields in autumn—

But where the deep plough furrowed the field
White steam arose from the rich red land
Incense and prayer for the harvest's yield.

And as she lay in purple grass on a sandy hillside—

And the gothic mullen walks in pale procession
Holding up faint torches to the sky.

Words came for a beech tree on a hill—

Old robes discarded, naked and fair,
And shook in the wind that swayed about her
A glory and wonder of red brown hair.

And for the street lamps shining along the street outside the
Church—

> Golden gleaming beads,
> On the pale throat of night.

She wrote in the repose of the evening when "work" for the day
was over. Or in the quiet and sometimes lonely recesses of solitude
that are part of a person who lives much of life outside the closed
intimacy of family.

Her poems disclose a human being who instinctively stepped out
into her back garden with the greatest care for fear of treading on
a bug.

"I believe this fly wants out," she was known to remark as she
picked a buzzing fly from the window in a friend's house and carefully released it out of doors.

The friend could easily have laughed, except that Florence was so
patently sincere.

"I love all animals—even man!" she once pronounced. Man with
his frailties could do wicked things; animals were part of nature
and so without evil. It was easy to love and care for animals. Animals and children. Time after time over the years there would be
a knock at the studio door.

"Miss Wyle, we found this bird on the road. It can't fly. Can you
help it?"

Birds, rabbits, turtles, cats, dogs from all over the neighbourhood
were trundled to her door in the supreme confidence that Miss Wyle
could make them well, or at least could deal with them. Sometimes
she could, and there would be great rejoicing. Sometimes it was
already dead, and another little grave would be added to the row
out in the garden.

The garden at the back of the Church was Florence's open line to
nature. In it she could watch the pattern of the seasons.

> The miracle of coming spring
>   breaks on the heart
> As sight on the eyes of a man
>   long blind.

In the forties this garden was still considered one of the most interesting natural gardens in the city. It was mostly rocks and ground cover and was cut off by trees from the noise of the city. Birds found it a haven. A peach tree climbed, vine-like, up the back of the Church, and even yielded a few peaches now and then. Visitors remember it with delight as a peaceful spot to sit and have tea with the Girls. In warm weather the S.S.C. relaxed there during meetings.

Earlier it had been more than delightful. It had been magnificent, especially in spring. A great slope of rock garden reached around to the back from above the driveway on the east side of the building. In spring it was a riot of wildflowers that the Girls had transplanted from the farm. The newspapers wrote it up annually—which brought hordes of people driving along the street, craning for a look at the wondrous pastel-hued bank. At first both of the Girls had worked at it, but Frances soon grew rather ungainly for the kind of bending that gardening entailed, and the garden became Florence's preserve.

During the war it was still in good shape, although perhaps edging more and more toward the wild. A garden to Florence never did mean a regular pattern of plantings; things more or less went in where convenient, with merely an aim for overall balance. She was not what would be considered a passionate gardener. She had too many other things to do. She simply liked to see things growing. And everything that Florence planted grew.

"It was hardly a garden as a cultivated garden is known," a frequent visitor recalled. "But cultivated in the sense that she loved it."

When Mount Pleasant Avenue was put through, bringing the shrill traffic noises only a few houses away, the Girls planted a row of poplars as a protective barrier. But the city was too much with them. Along with the noise a stale smell of oil and gasoline occasionally filtered through the trees. Many of the birds deserted for less civilized retreats.

As the years passed and Florence became less able to contain the growth a small jungle developed at the back of 110 Glenrose Avenue. Still, it remained, euphemistically, "the garden." Florence poked in it a good deal, moving things about, which appeared to stimulate them alarmingly. A tiny peach tree sprang up from a pit tossed at random. Numerous other tree seedlings rooted themselves, forming a kind of natural nursery. Forsythia and other shrubbery overgrew their beds in wild profusion. Eventually things tangled together, until only a small area of grass outside the back door was exposed to sunlight. The Girls often sat there.

Henrietta Banting found them doing so one very hot summer afternoon. It was a reasonably refreshing spot with a sort of forest cool emanating from the riotous growth. Frances was in her shorts —an incredible sight. Over to one side, emerging from the tangled shrubbery, Lady Banting was surprised to note a plaster head which was in an advanced stage of disintegration. Oh, the Girls explained, it had been the portrait of a man they had disliked very much—the president of some large concern who had been one of Frances' few disagreeable sitters. They considered it too charitable to smash the plaster and toss it away. For him, they decided on a slow demise—a kind of water torture washing him away in the summer rains.

Most people dropping by the studio on business would find Florence at work. Whether she was carving out in the garden, as she often was in summer, or in the studio, she kept regular hours. Unlike her partner, who was a fierce but sporadic worker, it was Florence's system to work every day, never to let a day go by without accomplishing something concrete and valid. "I guess I'm a puritan at heart after all," she acknowledged.

This respect for honest labour contributed to the rapport that Florence had with working men like John Murphy, who did their carting for many years. Indeed both Girls, as reflected in their various portraits of ashmen, miners, harvesters and the like, felt a strong affinity for working people. In return, most men recognized that when they went to the Church to do a job, they worked with the Girls, not for them. As John Murphy phrased it, "You were one of the crew."

Florence's unsophisticated nature, her simple directness, earned her special regard from such men. She would be up in the back of the truck helping John load a piece of sculpture, making sure it was well and safely packed. He would lean over to her and say in a low voice, "Florence, do you have your union card?" She, in turn, would feel in her pocket and answer conspiratorially, "No, I've misplaced it."

Florence Wyle's sculpture cannot be measured in terms of her commissions and public monuments. In most cases her best things were those that she quietly created from the urgings of her mind and her heart. They were like her children. "They are our immortality," she once told a young sculptor.

Sometimes they flowed out of the pages of a book she had read. She conceived one of her major works from a series of publications, *The Rivers of America*. Over several years in the forties, a series of carvings evolved, illustrating the great rivers of the American continents: the Mississippi, the Colorado, the St. Lawrence, the Rio Grande, the Amazon, ten in all, each interpreted as a curving, flowing, twisting form of a woman. They were carved in wood from the sumach tree, which with its striking purplish grain threading through the olive-coloured wood, almost simulated the current and flow of the river. Seen grouped together, as they were meant to be, the carvings gave a remarkable impression of flowing water.

Wood was living matter to a sculptor like Florence. There was always a pile of it in the corner of the studio—lengths of sumach, cherry, apple wood, their ends sealed with protective paraffin, drying slowly until they were finally ready for the probing chisel. To the unpractised eye the pile looked like fodder for the great maw of the fireplace. But to Florence the rough slabs and sections of small tree trunks represented sculptures waiting to be released. As a token of special regard she might dig one out when a promising young sculptor dropped by the Church. "Here, see what you can do with this." And the young hopeful would head off to his own studio, the prize under his arm, ideas turning in his head.

She herself handled each rough piece with reverence. Choosing a length to suit the design at hand, she would begin with her tools: wooden hammer, an assortment of chisels, and even an unorthodox jacknife. She felt her way slowly, cutting lightly, exploring the possibilities of the grain, establishing key points, adapting her inspiration to the nature of the material. Caressing the wood with her tools, slowly she would uncover a nebulous head. The curve of an incised backbone would follow the grain and set the design in motion. Rhythm and balance would come into play with the swelling of breast and a thigh, suddenly the pulse would begin to beat, and a sculpture emerged from the wood.

Regrettably, the "Rivers," perhaps the finest examples of Florence's direct carving, were not to remain intact as a composite work. Although they were exhibited a number of times and were always highly acclaimed, no one showed the foresight to purchase them as an entity. In the end she relented before pressure to break the series, and sold the carvings separately.

One of her finest works was the result of a sudden release of accumulated social convictions. It all came to a head during a class she was teaching in the Church. A young Negro woman was modelling for the students, and as Florence moved about, overseeing the various efforts, she was overcome by a surge of feeling about the plight of the Negro.

On an impulse she set to work alongside the students, modelling a life-size head and torso of the woman. The result was an extremely beautiful, earthy figure, strongly modelled so that the pose of the arms and the hands, the neck and the head all harmonized to express the pride and dignity and force and determination of man, and his right to equality as a human being.

Strangely, the public at the time seemed to consider it propaganda. "Well, they were away off," was Florence's disgusted reaction. Besides, as she noted with ironic humour, really very few people noticed it at all when it was on public exhibition. Although considered one of her best efforts the "Negro Woman" never sold.

Most of Florence's work was of the nude figure. "That's what I think about when I think of sculpture—the figure."

She had studied the human figure in detail for so many years at art school that she very seldom used a model for her designs. She did not need one. Her knowledge of bone and muscle and curve and proportion gave her great freedom of movement, which in turn surfaced as that quality of fluidity which is common to all her works. Even as the changing trends began to eliminate the figure from sculpture, she never lost her reverence for the human form. "The reason I've done almost all of these things, I suppose, is

81

because I think that the human animal is a beautiful one," she once said.

One evening, a friend brought along, to a studio gathering, a guest who was accustomed to making remarks deliberately designed to stir up controversy. On this occasion he stated loudly, for all to hear, that he thought portraits had to be nude studies if the real character of a subject was to be revealed. As he paused, waiting for a shocked reaction, he was somewhat shocked himself to have Florence step in with an immediate "You're absolutely right! Absolutely!"

Florence had little regard for clothes as an adornment for the human figure. Fashion repelled her, although her artist's eye had to acknowledge harmony when she saw it in a person's dress. Her own uniform consisted of baggy grey flannel pants of questionable vintage and heavy shoes that appeared to have been made for a man. And somewhere, usually, a touch of blue—a scarf, or a shirt of pale blue flannel or cotton. It was her colour.

Sculptor Dora de Pedery Hunt dropped by one day on her way to an exhibition opening, and Frances remarked that she looked very distinguished. Florence, who was nearby, put in, "What is distinguished? Dora looks all right. But distinguished? I really don't like that expression. I wouldn't want to be distinguished"

Frances said very quietly, "Florence, no matter what you do, you are distinguished."

"*Firenze*," Charles Ashley had called her.

Over the years she only appeared once in truly feminine apparel. It was the established custom for the Girls to have New Year's dinner with friends, the Bernard Radleys. Florence arrived one year in a dress of soft, summery material, with a full skirt and tight waist. On her head was a large picture hat, and over one ear, a rose. She was absolutely stunning. But evidently she considered that such frippery did not mix with the real business of life, which was work, for the costume was never seen again. It was almost as though she felt she was betraying the cause if she allowed herself any of the frivolities of the so-called weaker sex.

Both Girls were ardent feminists, and Florence fiercely so. They considered it ridiculous that professional titles should designate sex.

Sculptress? Why should there be sculptresses any more than "doctresses?" After all, they themselves had proven that women were able to excel in this demanding profession that had traditionally been considered a man's field. Without any beating of drums they resolved the discrimination by systematically referring to themselves and their female colleagues as sculptors. Since they backed their defiance with solid accomplishment, it had a positive effect.

The two of them differed, however, in that Frances made no bones about being very fond of men. She was a compulsive flirt. Florence, on the other hand, always pretended to dislike men and often cited the case of her twin brother. When they were children she had excelled him in most tasks, yet he had always managed somehow to garner the praise. She seemed never to recover from those early injustices. But when it came down to reality, she disliked men except for those she liked—which included most of the men she knew. She exempted these from the blanket of general condemnation, but even they were no match for women. "I like men. But women do most things very much better!"

In later years her allergies were a burden to her and to anyone who had anything to do with her. She suffered terribly from them. Her face would puff out in red splotches and her sinuses would swell painfully. There were tests. The results indicated sensitivity to dust, cats and smoke. She chose to acknowledge only the smoke. After all, dust in a sculptor's studio where clay and plaster were in constant use was absolutely unavoidable. Cats—well, she could not blame the beloved cats. Smoke she found offensive anyway, so smoke became the token sacrifice.

Frances took it very seriously. She had been a chain smoker for years, as her hacking cough confirmed. But her concern for Florence was such that she stopped smoking immediately, and insisted that guests who had to smoke retire downstairs to do so.

For Florence, her allergies provided a perfect excuse to retire completely from any sort of public life. She appeared rarely at public events from then on, claiming that it was to avoid smoke. But for a long while she had felt that the public side of the art world, social gatherings, openings, the repetitive squabbling at society meetings, had very little to do with art. Time was beginning to close in on her and she seemed to have decided to devote her remaining energies to what she valued most in life. She was criticized for it and inevitably there was a bit of fun poked at her. However she had no time to fret over criticism; there were more important things to consider. The problem was to find enough hours in a day for all the things she wanted to do.

Three indelible images remain with people who knew Florence well. First and always is the image of her at work. Second and third are the images of her growing things and caring for animals.

In their old age an interviewer asked the Girls how they would define happiness. Frances hesitated, to compose her thoughts, but Florence was able to answer immediately. "I should think several pet dogs."

It was always a problem to restrain her from sending off substantial contributions to the Humane Society, regardless of the financial situation at the Church. Stray animals were definitely encouraged to linger.

The Girls' good friend, veterinarian Edith Williams, came to know Florence's impulses from close range. She had had a nodding acquaintance with the two of them for a long time, and then one day Florence telephoned her to ask if she could come along to see a sick cat. She had never seen them professionally before, but knew that they were aware of her work because people had brought animals to her office explaining, "Miss Wyle sent me to you."

Dr. Williams went along on this particular afternoon and shortly found herself in the midst of the most unusual conditions that she had ever encountered in her practice of veterinary medicine. Florence answered the door, as usual, and ushered her into what seemed a chaotic scene in the studio. Actually it was only Frances teetering on top of a ladder, working away furiously on a monumental sculpture. The cat in question was sitting on top of another ladder. Florence suggested, "I think if you look at it up there, it wouldn't be disturbed."

So there was nothing for it but to climb the ladder to examine the cat—which, it turned out, was only suffering from indigestion. At that moment the doorbell buzzed, and a young reporter from one of the Toronto papers was shown in to join the group. He had come for an interview on the latest doings of the Sculptors' Society. Frances, always the spokesman at such times, went right on rasping away and making a great noise, while at the same time alternately shouting directions to Dr. Williams about the cat and calling down to the reporter about the S.S.C.

Florence insisted that they must all have tea, and off she went to make it. She brought it up from the kitchen on a tray, but noting that she had forgotten something, set the tray on a low table and hurried back downstairs. Immediately two cats sprang up and began drinking out of the milk pitcher. The young man looked at Dr. Williams in horror and then was struck by a fit of laughter. It became infectious, uncontrollable. When it finally subsided, they had their tea, without milk.

From then on Edith Williams was called in often over the years. Florence did not have as much absolute faith in her own medical ability as the neighbourhood children. Assorted animals—cats, stray dogs, even pigeons—were the patients.

One stray dog that Florence had been feeding would not allow itself to be caught. The Girls felt sure it had been maltreated and was therefore afraid of people. They decided to solicit professional help. Dr. Williams was called, and on her arrival chased the animal dutifully in and out of various backyards until it finally dashed into one yard and stayed there. She had just cornered it and was leading it away when the mistress of the house appeared at the back door to inquire with some ire, "Where are you taking my dog?"

Neighbours were perhaps justifiably indignant that their well-fed, well-cared-for cats and dogs were sometimes placed in the category of strays. The animals, on the other hand, loved it. Quite a number took advantage of the welcome mat at the Church and made daily stops of their own accord.

Florence feeding her animals. A strong image.

But even stronger, Florence at work. Sculpture flowed endlessly from her gnarled fingers. The work was now hard labour, physically, as well as a constant drain on inner strength. By the end of the forties she was suffering from arthritis and a heart condition, but even more from the gnawing realization that although she and

Frances were accorded the greatest personal respect in art circles, tides of interest were quickly moving out, isolating their work as a thing of the past. She conceded little to these stones in her path, but her poetry reflects the dreariness they brought her.

> My feet are broken with striving
> My hands are broken with pain,
> My soul is broken with knowledge,
> Yet must I circle again
> These dim ways
> Leading to darkness.

But her beloved garden was always there to compose her spirit.

> I will not feed my soul with sorrow,
> Not while dark trees march in naked majesty
> Across the sun set sky.

CHAPTER

8

The years were catching up with both of the Girls, but it was a long while before they considered resigning themselves to the disability of old age.

Frances, as always, had a great many pots stewing on the fire in the early fifties. One brew, prepared for her old friend Robert Flaherty, looked most promising—a savoury mixture of artistic banner-waving, overdue recognition, and an honest use of talent.

Since his earlier days in Toronto, Flaherty had made a respected name for himself as a pioneer in documentary films. But his accomplishments had never been widely acclaimed in Canada, where he had developed his early work. Frances, who was a tireless champion of the talents of her friends, thought it a great waste when work of persons of great ability went unrecognized. So when the opportunity arose, she pursued the suggestion that, under the auspices of the National Gallery, an invitation might be sent to Flaherty to develop a series of documentaries on various Canadian subjects.

Correspondence flew thick and fast between Frances and H. O. McCurry, and the idea emerged that Flaherty might undertake a sort of pilot film centred on the Girls and their work, to initiate the series. Everyone was thrilled. Flaherty himself was enthused. Frances astounded everyone by going on a diet—the first and only time she was ever known to do so.

But unfortunately for Canada, for Flaherty, and for the Girls, funds for the series failed to materialize, and not even the initial film was made. And Flaherty's death a few years later cut short the hope of reviving the project.

If they could not have the satisfaction of seeing belated credit directed toward a longstanding colleague in the arts, at least the Girls could pursue their interest in the struggles of emerging artists. Frances and Florence were the first professionals to accept many young sculptors as colleagues.

Frances Gage was in her last year at the Ontario College of Art when she first came in contact with the Girls. The Sculpture Department at the College, headed by Emmanuel Hahn, did not at that time acknowledge the Girls' existence, and students were usually unaware of them.

But as it happened, Frances Gage had come to know Edith Williams, the veterinarian and Dr. Freda Fraser, with whom Edith lived. "You haven't met the Girls?" Edith asked Frances somewhat incredulously, and immediately invited her to dinner with the two legendary figures.

Frances Gage was not quite prepared for the Girls. Few people ever were. This time Frances Loring, always in the vanguard, appeared in the Fraser-Williams garden sporting a pair of elephant-sized green trousers. (Despite her dieting she was still immense.) She was walking with the support of one cane, while her other hand was holding her old brown coat which trailed along on the ground behind her. A tacky green beret was pulled rakishly down to one side of her head. Florence brought up the rear, tottering along, dressed for the dinner outing in her old grey suit. Neat enough except for the heavy stockings which drooped in wrinkles around her ankles. Frances Gage realized immediately that she was in the presence of two very great personalities.

Understandably, she felt diffident, a condition that persisted even at the dinner table. She politely declined the offer of a second helping. "Have another," ordered Florence. "Artists eat when they can!"

The dinner party was the beginning of a long and happy association that saw Frances Gage in and out of the Church regularly for the next eighteen years.

The year 1952 was significant for a number of reasons. Florence was seventy years of age, and with the old age pension coming in, the Girls decided that the time had come when they could afford regular household help.

And so Agnes came to them. Agnes Boehmke had been a book-keeper in Germany, but lacking a fluent grasp of English, could not hope for work in her own field. On impulse she answered the ad in the paper and shortly found herself having tea with the Girls and discussing the prospect of working for them. The experience proved quite unnerving for her. (She had never been in an artist's studio before.) The Girls were their usual cheerful, friendly selves, however, and all went quite well until they took her downstairs to show her the kitchen and washing area. Lying here and there in the semi-darkness around the octopus of a furnace, were pieces of plaster casts—arms, heads and legs that had been left after abortive castings. Agnes was seized with terror. The story of Hansel and Gretel flashed through her mind.

"But I got used to it," she said later, with a shrug. She stayed with them until the end.

Later that same spring the Girls came to a major decision. The balance of the gravel money from the farm was still intact. They would use it to build a separate studio wing for Florence. Workmen arrived to cut down trees late in June. By August, Frances reported complete chaos at the studio. Building operations had begun and the walls were nearly up, but both entrances were temporarily blocked. Frances remarked, regretfully, "I haven't reduced quite enough for the window we have to use."

The construction period was very frustrating for Florence, the expert craftsman. She could hardly bear to watch their slipshod methods and disorganized movements. "They climb over a pile of concrete blocks sixty-two times a day rather than move them. It would only take two minutes to move the silly things," she wrote to their friend Mrs. H. A. Dyde in Edmonton. But she conceded, "Well, well. I guess I am too orderly."

In the midst of all this confusion came an extremely exciting proposal for Frances. Under the joint sponsorship of the National Gallery and the University of Alberta, she and A. Y. Jackson were invited to tour the towns and villages of Alberta's Peace River District, giving art lectures at each stop. They left on October 15th for two weeks, and travelled as far west as the beginning of the Alaska Highway at Dawson Creek, and as far north as the town of Peace River. They travelled by car once they reached the West, and were conducted throughout by the province's representative for cultural affairs, Blake MacKenzie.

The trip was an exhilarating experience for Frances, who had always had such faith in the North. In all, they covered 1,200 miles, through territory where people had had little opportunity for contact with artists. She was deeply moved by the hunger for knowledge that she found. There were far more questions from the young people of that remote area than from the informed and well-off audiences that she was used to encountering at home.

Frances grumbled laughingly for years afterwards that A.Y., as she affectionately called him, always managed to upstage her by taking the platform first. Since he was a fascinating but garrulous talker, the audience would be restive by the time Frances got up to speak. At the end of one evening, A.Y. warmly congratulated her on her talk, saying that he had never heard her speak so well.

"No wonder!" Frances said when she repeated the story later. "It was the first chance I'd had to speak first and with enough time to develop my theme properly!"

She was full of admiration for the patience Jackson had for the amateur painters who came along with their work. He was extremely kind in his criticism and tried to give the sort of practical suggestions that must have meant a great deal to amateurs. And she marvelled at his empathy with children. "He seems to enter right into their minds."

The travellers experienced one wild night on the way to the town of High Prairie. They were still on the road after dark and inadvertently hit a large bump. They did not realize until later that the trunk of the car had sprung open and Jackson's suitcase, MacKenzie's dunnage bag, and Frances' sculpture photos had been thrown out somewhere along the route. When the loss was discovered they turned back to retrace their tracks, logging up several hundred extra miles before they gave up hope of sighting their belongings. A.Y. was quite concerned, as it meant that he was left with only the clothes on his back. They rolled into High Prairie and their hotel, empty-handed, at 6:45 in the morning.

Frances took it all in her stride. A few hours later she wrote a report of the adventure to Mrs. Dyde in Edmonton. "The frail ones are still sleeping but I have had my breakfast—my tummy says breakfast at nine no matter what." Despite the strain of the hectic night she seemed to have suffered no ill effects. "Such a beautiful night it was, though—I really am not a bit tired."

The time spent with the school children on their route seemed the most worthwhile to Frances. Wherever they spoke, busloads of students were brought in to hear them. These young people were so eager that Frances began to have reservations about the value of the trip. "It is all very well to stir up their interest, but where do they go from there?"

The trip itself, however, confirmed her belief in the North. "It wouldn't be surprising if something remarkable came from that area," she predicted on her return to Toronto. "The artistic youth hasn't been moulded by older ideas. Something strong and truly native to the country should spring from northwestern Alberta."

Back at the studio, there had been alarming developments. Fire had broken out in the new wing, leaving considerable damage. Slipshod methods again. The workmen had piled scrap material in the new fireplace, against Florence's explicit advice, and touched a match to it. The scrap blazed up and set fire to the wall between the new and the old studios. Frances Gage happened to be on her way to the Church at the time, and arrived to find firemen swarming all over the roof with axes. They had broken through the skylight and smoke was billowing out in a cloud. Others were forcibly holding Florence back from trying to re-enter the church for Petey the cat. Petey, as it turned out, had retreated to safety in the basement.

The fire chief made quite a hit with Florence. And no wonder. Before the fire was out he had directed men into the studio with great tarpaulins to cover all the sculpture. So that, in spite of soaking the whole place with water, no major works were seriously harmed.

It had been a time of extreme agitation for Florence, but she had recovered her normal serenity by the time Frances was due back from the West. She drove out to the airport with friends to meet the two travellers.

Frances was very tired, and nursing a nasty cold. Even A.Y. was silent. He confessed later to having talked more out West than he ever had in his life. Of the three of them, Florence seemed to have best survived the travails of the two-week period. Frances wrote back to Mrs. Dyde, "Florence seems to have had a good time—which indicates she needs more excitement. Hope she doesn't realize it and start more excitement."

The fire had caused considerable structural damage but it was made good by the architect. The Girls never did consider the design of the wing to be anything more than functionally adequate. At first they had jokingly threatened to dig a moat around it and christen it "The Citadel." But when it was completed it suited them very well. Provision had been made for a good-sized casting room in the basement, which they never did use much, accustomed as they were to making do with primitive equipment.

The new studio was a great success though. A huge window faced north and flooded Florence's work space with a subdued greenish light that reflected from the lush growth in the garden outside. Within a very short time the room took on the tones and lights and shadows of her personality. She worked there contentedly throughout her remaining active years. It became a maze, crowded with various sculptures and work paraphernalia, so that she herself was sometimes almost obscured as she carved and modelled away. But it was a structured maze. There was order in the seeming disorder, calm in the careful confusion. No one entered that maze without being touched by the tranquillity of spirit that permeated the area. It was like a quiet refuge from the tumult of the world, from which one came away strangely renewed.

The new arrangement was also very pleasant for Frances, for as time passed she was forced by her disabilities into longer and longer periods of physical inactivity, which were bound to conflict with a work atmosphere. She occupied herself more and more with business related to sculpture and art in general, often making great use of the telephone. The main studio was still the centre of the home, so to speak, and nothing was changed except that each could follow her gradually diverging inclinations without always having to consider whether she was getting into the other's environment.

The parties, sadly but inevitably, had come to an end, but there were still a great many people in and out of the Church. Meetings were held there from time to time but were awkward because of Florence's allergy. The different sculptors came by frequently for one thing or another. And, happily, the Girls were now in a position to indulge themselves more liberally if they came by for assistance. They were so secretive about this last, though, that the extent of their aid can never be fully assessed. They were aware that from time to time they were being done by some of their more unfortunate associates, but they did not feel that this rendered the offenders any less needy.

The intellectual level in the Church remained consistently high and the social environment consistently heterogeneous. It was not unusual for a friend happening by at tea time to find himself sitting down around the fireplace with anyone from the latest casualty with a hard luck story to a diplomat or Cabinet minister. Frances would sit on the couch, vivid with charm, intelligence, and sometimes wicked humour. Florence, alternately pithy or warmly earthy in her comments, clumped about in her heavy shoes, doing the tea honours.

Even at this late stage the neighbourhood in general seemed not to know that anything of special note went on in the Church. There had been strong local objections when the new wing was proposed —particularly, for some obscure reason, when the sewers were connected. The newer residents had thought, hitherto, that the eyesore would dilapidate itself out of existence. But sewers seemed so very permanent. When objections had been overruled and construction completed, property-conscious residents on the street were somewhat placated to see a coat of respectable pale grey paint being brushed over the old red of the Church.

The pigeons were another matter. Pigeons had long nested on the roof of the old studio—rather precariously. Keith was often summoned from his shack behind the Studio Building to rig up safer nesting places with wire and wood. Sometimes these broke down under the wear and tear of successive generations, tumbling the eggs to a violent end below, much to the Girls' distress. But on the whole, the pigeons prospered and led what must have been a very pleasant life, visiting back and forth among the nearby roofs.

Understandably, they became a source of great annoyance to everyone but the Girls. When an immediate neighbour reshingled his roof with dark blue asphalt tile—most unwise—he was not at all amused at the constant disfigurement and discoloration. Complaints aimed at routing out the pigeons were airily dismissed by the Girls with perfect seriousness. "Really, it's very simple," Frances offered, in her tone of ultimate rationalism." You should just paint your roof all white!" The pigeons, defended with such unanswerable logic, were reprieved for the time being.

Certainly there was a great deal of solid accomplishment generated in the Church in the early fifties, but at a reduced tempo. Frances soon let up on her dieting and became larger than ever— well over 200 pounds. No large commissions loomed on the horizon to challenge her increasing size and immobility, so she channelled her efforts toward improving the lot of sculptors by working on committees.

She served on the Art Gallery of Toronto purchasing committee for some years, with men like A. J. Casson, Charles Comfort and Charles Band. All three men found it a unique and stimulating experience to work with Frances Loring. The two painters had known her well for many years, and were not unprepared for her crusading spirit. But it could not have been easy to serve with her. Her integrity was impregnable, and she upheld her principles, and her prejudices, unequivocally. Nothing that she disapproved of got by without her raising "a damned good fuss" about it. Yet she was so untainted by personal opportunism that her judgment was immensely respected. Any opposition she made was heartfelt and was backed by intelligent appraisal so that it never seemed to raise the ire of dissenting committee members. She did not mind stepping on peoples' toes, but tried to do so diplomatically whenever possible.

Except when it came to dealing with Martin Baldwin, the gallery's director. She and Baldwin battled constantly. Frances was far from being a yes-man, and when she and some of the others felt that Baldwin was being over-influenced by prevailing American trends, she left him in no doubt as to her thoughts on the matter. Baldwin retaliated with ammunition from his own verbal arsenal, but his weapons fell far short of the mark. Frances snorted back at him on one heated occasion, with reference to his long-established family background, "It would take more than either a Martin or a Baldwin to put down a Loring!"

Her presence on any committee—Art Gallery, Sculptors' Society, Royal Academy, Ontario Society of Artists—was enough to ensure fair play on any issue. As time went by, some of the younger people began to find her integrity a decided obstacle. Her stands on points of principle were enough to drive young schemers to distraction. Anyone who wished to get around her had to be clever indeed. One sculptor managed to do so undetected. He usually connived to manoeuvre himself into position for counting the ballots in S.S.C. elections—and so constituted himself a one-man jury.

For Florence it was work as usual. During this period it was she who was busy with commissions. Several things came along that suited her talents perfectly: two or three fountain figures, and a relief featuring farm animals for the Ontario Veterinary College in Guelph. She described them as "typical farm animals, not thoroughbreds, but good stock—horses, cows, dogs, ducks, gulls—good earthy creatures."

And although these works were all things that she wanted to do, she admitted the strain. "Sometimes one just gets too tired to go on, but a detective story and a warm bed at night help me a lot." The warm bed was in reference to the gift of an electric blanket the previous Christmas, while detective stories had long been her only outright concession to relaxation.

But the Calvert Trophies commission was enough to rouse both Girls to full potential. It all began when Calvert Distillers, sponsors of the Dominion Drama Festival, decided that trophies should be presented to the winners from various regions. At precisely this time Laing Galleries on Bloor Street happened to have Florence's "Rivers of America" series on display, and the Festival's trophy committee of two, Pauline McGibbon and David Ongley, were directed down to have a look at these wooden sculptures. They decided immediately that carvings of a similar nature would make a stunning trophy series.

The Girls were approached. On that first visit Mrs. McGibbon joined the ranks of those who found themselves not altogether prepared for the Church and its occupants. She could not help but notice that "cleanliness was not one of the prime requisites as far as their lives were concerned." But, as usual, the Girls' diverting personalities soon drew attention away from chips of wood in the teacups and bits of plaster on the cake.

As there were a considerable number of trophies involved, the commission was finally divided among Florence, Frances and Sylvia Daoust from Montreal. Florence was assigned the particular honour of carving the top Festival award, "Drama."

Frustratingly, wood was not available locally and had to be ordered from a hardwood outlet in New York. Whitewood, tulip wood and mahogany. The three sculptors waited with anticipation for word of its arrival. None came. Letters of inquiry brought confirmation that the order had been shipped as specified. They waited a while longer. Still no wood and no clue as to its whereabouts. The entire shipment had completely disappeared somewhere en route. A tracer was put on it through border customs, and finally an extensive search unearthed the wood in the corner of a customs shed—packed in old onion bags. They had been set aside for fumigation. While the soft bags made excellent coverings for the wood, onions had evidently suffered a blight that year, and nothing connected with them was allowed across the border without being decontaminated.

Florence and Frances, both full of aches and pains, were soon happily at work, following the grain in the wood with hammer and chisel. "F. and I have both been pretty busy for elderly ladies (ha! ha!)," Florence quipped in a letter, never dreaming that anyone would take the elderly lady part seriously.

David Ongley and Pauline McGibbon had the very pleasant duty of checking on the progress of the trophies, checking rather more frequently than was necessary. Any excuse to visit the Girls. In fact, as they came to know the special tastes of Frances and Florence, they usually arrived with two contrasting offerings under their arms: vanilla ice cream and rye whiskey.

The trophies stirred up a serious political controversy. "The Governor-General downgraded for a liquor concern!" ran hysterical letters to the newspapers. The core of the trouble sprang from the significance of the previous top award in the Dominion Drama Festival, the Bessborough Trophy, which had been graciously donated by Lord Bessborough when he was Governor-General, back in the days of the Depression. Now it was being retired from its original role and awarded instead for the best classical play. Ousted, the critics claimed, by the new Calvert Trophy. These insinuations were a source of acute regret to those involved with the series of distinguished new trophies.

Then Vincent Massey, who was Governor-General at the time, quietly let it be known that he would attend the final festival scheduled for that year in Victoria, B.C. On the night of the ceremony he himself presented the controversial awards, and by this simple gesture stamped them with unreserved approval. There were no voices raised against them when they were subsequently exhibited across the country.

The trophies followed the festival circuit for nearly twenty years, until, due to wear and tear of the wood sculptures, they were retired before they became permanently disfigured.

That same year of the Calvert Trophies, 1953, Florence was honoured by long overdue official acknowledgement of her years of devotion to her art. She was awarded a Coronation Medal for, rather curiously, her "distinguished place as a member of Canadian art societies." She could no longer answer, as she had done earlier when queried as to what awards had come her way, "Not much of any, although I once got a ten dollar prize for a wallpaper design."

The following year Frances received the University of Alberta's national award, "for long and conspicuous service to the arts." The ceremonies were held at Banff, which entailed another trip west for Frances. She used the occasion to spend a week or so at a quiet resort in the mountains. The breather was to stand her in good stead. For, at sixty-seven years of age, her immense bulk half-crippled, she was on the brink of the most spectacular chapter in her long career.

CHAPTER

9

The sculpture on Parliament Hill?

"Unfortunately, Parliament Hill has a certain number of sculptural atrocities."

The National War Memorial?

"Cheap melodrama—which means that when a person looks at it, they want to rush away and never look at it again."

As various persons had found throughout the years, it was unwise to solicit Frances Loring's opinion unless one truly wished to have her considered answer.

The opportunity eventually came for her to give substance to her criticisms, to show what she herself could do.

It was in February of 1953 that the Federal Parliament in Ottawa approved in principle a commission for the tenth portrait-statue to be erected on Parliament Hall—that of Robert Borden. At the end of March, Prime Minister Louis St. Laurent announced an open competition to be administered by the National Gallery, and offered the winning contestant $50,000 to carry out the commission.

For Frances it was like a clarion call to battle.

With the utmost thoroughness, she set about assimilating everything there was to know about Robert Borden: the public statesman, the private individual, his physical characteristics, his ideals. In her quest she came across his memoirs. "I suppose I have to wade through them," she thought. She plunged into them dutifully, only to find them a most fascinating account of the times she too had lived through. The photographs had given a visual understanding of her subject; the memoirs now provided an insight into his thoughts. A common chord had been struck. She began to feel a certain affinity with Robert Borden.

The competition called for the submission of maquettes representing the sculptor's concept of the proposed finished work. Frances, never one to stint on effort, submitted two fourteen-inch clay replicas.

Restrictions were few. Generally, the monument had to fit into the Victorian style of Parliament Hill, and in particular, it had to balance the Laurier monument which flanked the Parliament Buildings on the opposite side of the hill. The challenge was to come up with a convincing likeness of Borden in a style that would not conflict with the existing surroundings.

Frances was very firm about her point of departure. "Almost every statesman on Parliament Hill is standing with his weight on one foot and his hand in the air, his first finger pointing upwards. I was determined that Borden was not going to stand on one hip, and he was not going to have his hand up in the air."

Her first model did not please her. She had Borden wearing a Prince Albert—a politician's garb of the day—but it was rather a boring garment from the standpoint of a sculptor. The dullness of dress constricted the possibilities for sculptural design and toned down the effect of dignity and intellectual force that were part of the man.

Her friend Vera Parsons, a Toronto lawyer, was at the studio one evening. The two of them walked round and round the model of Borden, reconstructing in their minds the background of the Parliament Buildings against which it would be seen when—and if—it was finally in place.

Frances was far from satisfied. She had caught a credible likeness of her subject and he was indeed "standing firmly on both feet." But she was trying for more than that. She wanted to catch the fighting Borden that had seen Canada through the First World War, a Borden that could hold his own against the grand Victorian background.

Suddenly Vera Parsons had a brainwave. Men of Borden's period had worn long great-coats. Why not swing one from around Borden's shoulders?

Frances grabbed up a heavy cloth and began arranging it over the shoulders of the model. It worked. The solid silhouette effect of the improvised great-coat gave the sense of drama that evoked the needed essence of vitality in the design. The following day she set about developing a second model in clay. It showed Borden in the great-coat, holding the Seals of Autonomy, a reminder that Canadian self-government had been extended to include autonomy in foreign affairs during his term as Prime Minister. Both models were entered in the competition, along with the entries of thirty-two other contestants.

For the thirty-three participating sculptors, this preliminary work had been a gamble. Only one of the lot could receive the final commission, although each of the six runners-up would be compensated for their effort by awards of $300.

The sketch models were to be in by October 31st. After what amounted to a moratorium that lasted five months, two people received notification indicating there was still life in the project. Frances Loring and sculptor Jean Meroz of Montreal were asked to submit models twice the size of their originals—at their own expense. The judges wished to consider these entries in fuller detail.

Frances' larger model (of Borden in the great-coat) reached the National Gallery in June. The two models were viewed by the officials in October. The jury reconvened in December. Three weeks later the Gallery advised the Prime Minister of the jury's recommendation of Frances Loring's model as winner of the competition.

"There is general gratification in the art world that the important national commission has gone to a sculptor of Frances Loring's artistic stature," ran the comment by art critic Pearl McCarthy in *The Globe and Mail*.

Frances received the honour with her usual equanimity and honesty. Viewing all the models afterwards she realized that one reason she had won the competition was because her design did fit in with the statue of Laurier, and it did fit in with Parliament Hill. "A lot of others may well have been better designs as monuments, but they didn't belong just there."

She was mistaken, actually. From the very first, only her second model and that of Jean Meroz had been under serious consideration. And of these two, that of Meroz was felt to be the more exciting as a sculptural design, but Frances' Borden in the great-coat had caught the essential spirit of the man.

With almost superhuman effort Frances pulled herself together (a sizeable feat) and rose above the pain of her heavy, dragging limbs. There was a time of brief but very real panic when she found out that the authorities were having second thoughts about their decision. It had come to their attention that Frances' physical condition was questionable, to say the least. But she knew perfectly well that she would be capable of carrying through with the job, and told them so. The authorities contented themselves by taking out a special insurance policy on Frances, covering their interests until such a time as the work had reached a conclusive stage.

Although this development was utterly galling to Frances, reminding her as it did that she was old, the bitterness of the pill was sweetened by an unexpected award. She was granted an honorary degree of Doctor of Laws from the University of Toronto in recognition of her outstanding contribution to the arts. "Throughout her life an active and faithful servant of the arts, an eloquent interpreter of Canada's history, a creator of lasting beauty," the citation read. The award set the juices flowing again in her old joints. Back to work. The perfect antidote to age.

The first phase of the undertaking was the building of a clay model one-half the size of the 9′ 7″ proposed finished work. There was no way around this disciplined approach to the job, for while the basic composition had been set in the original maquette, there was still a great deal of essential design to be finalized. Details, brought into focus by the larger scale, would have to be balanced and integrated with the existent forms. For once work on the massive bulk of the final figure had started, it would be technically almost impossible to adjust the design except in superficial areas. Major problems had to be solved before that crucial stage. The half-size model was the battleground in which masses and forms were pushed and shoved and forced into place until they harmonized.

The figure was built up nude. This was the usual method in the step-by-step development of a portrait statue; there is nothing more unconvincing than clothes draped over a dubious understructure.

Technical problems did develop as Frances worked. One stemmed from the fact that Borden had an unusually large head, which if depicted literally, would have resulted in an imbalanced statue. She resolved this by adding height to his legs, so that the whole seemed in proportion. Another difficulty arose over the great-coat that had been found so essential to the design. Halfway through, it was decided that a man in an overcoat was improperly dressed to be carrying anything so precious as the Seals of Autonomy. After some consideration, an acceptable adjustment was worked out. Borden was allowed instead to hold a small scroll representing a brief he had carried to the 1919 Peace Conference in Paris.

As the figure progressed, visitors to the Church were greeted by a sight that caused them to gasp with apprehension as they stepped into the main studio.

In order to position herself at working level with the head of the statue, Frances had erected a makeshift scaffolding: two rickety step-ladders, spanned across their tops by a frail-looking plank. When A. J. Casson dropped by one day he was confronted by Frances, her two-hundred pound bulk swathed in a coverall, standing suspended in mid-air on the frail plank. The plank sagged in terrifying fashion.

Casson appealed in subdued alarm to Florence who was poking about nearby. "Florence!"

"If she's going to fall she'll bounce!" Florence assured him philosophically.

The half-size plaster was to be shipped down to New York, where it would be enlarged by expert technicians in a studio near the bronze foundry. However, Frances was not prepared to leave the very important and sensitive area of the actual head in the hands of technicians, however skilled. She modelled a separate gigantic head to be incorporated later into the full-sized work.

By April of the following year the clay models were ready to be viewed by the official committee, headed by Alan Jarvis, who had become Director of the National Gallery after McCurry's death. The go-ahead was given for Frances to proceed to the final stage of enlargement, and, to Frances' intense relief, the Department of Public Works was advised that it could safely cancel the humiliating special insurance policy. They were obviously convinced at last that Frances could finish the statue. As if there had been any doubt!

The time had come to call in Willie Fediow. Willie was a painter, and sculptor Pauline Redsell's husband. He was also an accomplished plaster caster. And in the case of Sir Robert, Frances felt that a truly professional job was required.

But as Willie inspected the clay model with a view to giving an estimate, he was bombarded by conflicting instructions from both Frances and Florence as to how the casting job should be approached.

He went home with his head in a whirl. "You know," he confessed to his wife, "I don't think I'm going to be able to do that thing if both of them are going to be standing there telling me what to do!"

"Well," said Pauline, who knew the Girls well, "why don't you tell them so?"

He did just that the next morning.

Frances and Florence immediately roared with laughter. "Thank heavens," they exclaimed, seeing a way out of the indefensible corner they had boxed themselves into. "We were hoping you'd shut us up. We would never have managed to do it on our own."

(Willie died just a little over a year later, and when Pauline held a memorial exhibition of his paintings the following spring, the Girls came to pay tribute—Florence in her old grey suit, Frances right behind in a dreadful old dress and an ancient, floppy hat, trailing a great bunch of forsythia from Florence's garden. All present deferred as though royalty had arrived. Willie would have cherished the scene.)

When the casting was complete, Frances went to New York to supervise the enlarging operation. Even at that stage Sir Robert's large head continued to pose problems. "Mr. Borden is progressing. I have put his head three inches higher and his feet one inch lower. Helps him," she reported to Alan Jarvis.

But when the time came for Frances to begin working on the figure herself, filling in the important details, pulling the whole together, she was struck by a painful eye ailment. There was nothing for it but to retire to bed in her hotel room and wait for the inflammation to subside. As time was pressing, she put in an urgent call for help to Florence in Toronto. Would she come down to carry on with the modelling of the detail? The buttons, the coat lapels, the shoes. By the time Frances was able to get back to work, Florence had filled in the detail. However, since her basic approach to modelling had always been one of understatement, as opposed to Frances' emphasis on drama, Frances had to contrive, tactfully, to add a little of her dash to Florence's sensitive tooling.

As the figure neared the final casting stage, when a special mould would be taken from the plaster and filled with molten bronze, Frances had to fight yet another battle with Ottawa. The government had decided that the statue had to correspond exactly and absolutely with the other monuments on Parliament Hill: the panellings of script on each facing of the base were deleted from the design. Frances stood her ground. The back and side panellings perhaps did not matter aesthetically; they could go. But the front—no! The central panel was an integral part of the total design of the monument, and she categorically refused to have it eliminated.

She won.

Louis Temporale, the carver, who had already erected the granite base for the figure in Ottawa, went down with his heavy truck to pick up the bronze at the foundry. Sir Robert was lashed into place on the wooden truck bed, and the tedious haul got underway. The shortest route north brought them to a point on the St. Lawrence River where crossing had to be made by ferry. The weather had suddenly turned very cold, and a freak storm rose, working the water into an alarmingly angry froth. The captain of the ferry remarked uneasily that he had never seen the St. Lawrence as rough. Nevertheless, they pitched their way out to open water. Halfway across, Temporale was convinced they would lose truck, statue and all, to the bottom, and he was intensely relieved when they berthed at the pier on the north shore.

When the truck rolled triumphantly into Ottawa, the authorities nearly fainted. No, the monument could not be erected four weeks before the scheduled date. Yes, the pedestal was ready. Yes, there was a protective and concealing boarding already around the site. Yes, police were on the grounds. No, they could not even accept delivery of the monument four weeks ahead of time. No directives existed to cover this extreme situation.

Frances was equally adamant. No, she would not have the statue transported to Toronto. No, she would not consider an alternative. Yes, she did insist that the sculpture remain in Ottawa, and if it had to be stored in the basement of a nearby building until protocol allowed it to be officially received, so be it. She would pay the additional charges involved.

Four weeks later, on the official receiving day, the men and equipment were brought back to Ottawa to erect the statue. This time everything fell into place. The great bronze was hoisted up by the truck's chain pulley and it hung perfectly plumb on the first attempt. Sir Robert was lowered onto his pedestal, and was then covered in cloth and boxed in to await the unveiling, as yet some weeks away.

On January 8, 1957, the dignitaries gathered together against the bleak background of Parliament Hill in winter. Borden's nephew, Henry Borden, was there to unveil the monument, under the scrutiny of the Prime Minister, the Governor-General, and an extensive array of Cabinet ministers, diplomats and assorted personages. The cord was pulled, and the concealing curtain dropped from around the figure.

There he stood as his designer had pictured him from the very first: on a rise overlooking Wellington Street, with the West Block of the Parliament Buildings etching in a noble backdrop. Sir Robert Borden, standing solidly on two feet, steadfast and strong, the swing of the great-coat adding action to intellect.

The praise was gratifying. Overwhelming. There were even a few murmurs, from among those who remembered Borden, that she had been almost too successful. She had, they pointed out, made Sir Robert interesting, something he himself had failed to do.

The commission had taken nearly three years to complete. When a final tally was made of expenses—transportation, broker's fees, bronzing, lettering, photographs, and storage—her net profit was only twenty-five per cent of the original competition prize. But in the final analysis her satisfaction must have been immense and her reward measured in more lasting wealth. For there is no doubt that Frances Loring's Borden is, as A. Y. Jackson later affirmed, "the finest thing on Parliament Hill."

10

In their old age, after a lifetime of pursuing the beauty of traditional forms, the Girls were forced to acknowledge that those tenets upon which they had built their life work were being pushed aside in the more sophisticated art circles. Collectors were bypassing them. Architects were no longer calling—even for advice. But the Girls could not, and would not, desert the principles they considered as true and valid in art and life. "Our work might be old-fashioned to some people. It isn't to us, or we wouldn't do it!"

Frances tried to understand. "I think people should experiment, be allowed to experiment." She knew the new work could not be summarily dismissed. Yet on the whole she doubted its genuineness. "Some of it is research work that may lead somewhere. But most of it is adult kindergarten work. They're having an awfully good time, and it's fun and it's humorous. But people in a hundred years from now aren't going to see any humour in rusted automobile fenders."

Florence could not bring herself to be dispassionate. "They bring in a heap of rubbish from the street, and set it up and call it modern sculpture. Doesn't sound very interesting to me."

Frances may well have completed the "best thing on Parliament Hill." Florence's work may well have been described by Pearl McCarthy in *The Globe and Mail* as "free, individualistic art in the classic tradition, and with a quiet, poetic feeling, so good that any institution which hasn't a big piece of it has a hole in its artistic history." But the fact remained that their work was excluded from major art events. If it was any comfort to them, there were many artists of their era being swept into the same corner.

Then, when important collectors finally did come to call, Florence managed to scuttle hopes, simply by being herself.

"Florence," Frances cautioned, "when that collector and his wife come to see our work this afternoon, try not to mention Henry Moore." The couple in question were serious art lovers. They were possibly considering the acquisition of a Loring or a Wyle to round out their collection, which included a number of works by Henry Moore.

"Henry Moore! Hmph!" answered Florence. "Why should I mention him and those distortions that pass for sculptures nowadays?"

The couple arrived at the appointed hour. Florence let them in, and was the sweet, agreeable, vague self that she usually was with strangers. She showed them around the studio, and things went well. From her seat among the pillows on the sagging couch, Frances directed the conversation along safe lines. But eventually a pause occurred.

"We are so fond of the work of Henry Moore," offered the collectors. "We consider him to be the sculptor of the century."

It was like flaunting a red flag in front of a bull. "Rubbish!" Florence pronounced. "I could never forgive him for boring holes through a figure!"

The collectors looked stunned. Frances quickly intervened with, "I don't agree with what Henry Moore says, particularly, but I agree with his right to say it. Miss Wyle prefers the classics."

The collectors were happy to give her another chance. "But Moore weds the technical skill of the best classic traditions with new basic concepts. Surely you agree?"

"Not at all!" maintained Florence, now thoroughly aroused. And she launched into a stern lecture on the merits of classic sculpture as opposed to the decent modern trends.

The chastisement was too much for the collectors. They left shortly, their sense of humour apparently not broad enough to take this sort of thing in their stride, and their faith in their judgment apparently not strong enough to meet the challenge Florence offered. They never returned. Frances was temporarily a little piqued with her partner, but soon recovered, and in recollection they found the incident amusing.

"They probably wouldn't have bought anything anyway," Florence said.

Nevertheless, a few works by the Girls were making their way to prestigious homes. Florence's studies of F. H. Varley and A. Y. Jackson were among the first to go. Both had been modelled years before—Varley in 1922, and Jackson in 1943. There had never been enough funds to cast them in bronze and the plaster models had long been familiar as part of the backdrop in the studio. They were both excellent likenesses, and it was very gratifying to Florence when the National Gallery ordered bronze copies of each. At the time of the purchase, Florence reminisced about A.Y.'s sittings. During one of them he fell asleep, and as she recalled, "I didn't get very far that day. In any case, his usual way of posing was to hide behind a newspaper!"

Frances too, still powered by the momentum generated by her Borden effort, decided to have her large "Eskimo Woman and Child" done in more permanent material. She carved the final quarter-inch of the stone herself. Again there were fearful gasps at the sight of Frances perched with grand unconcern on that thin plank suspended between the two step-ladders. The work was almost beyond her, but she managed somehow to complete it, insisting, "I like manual labour, by George!" It was the last she did.

In 1960 an interested and influential party persuaded the National Gallery to add the "Eskimo Woman and Child" to its collection. It was included that summer in the gallery's annual selection of Canadian art to be sent to the Venice Biennale.

Florence, in spite of uncertain health, was remarkably busy during the late fifties. She carved a large marble torso for the Art Gallery of Toronto and modelled one of her finest baby figures for a small fountain in Counsell Garden in London, Ontario. "Florence Wyle's sculpture excels in the Counsell Garden," Pearl McCarthy remarked in a column. "She is considered by some the best sculptor in the country, always achieving a lyrical poetic ease in form." Welcome praise in the midst of the changing art climate.

A small volume of her poems was published in 1959. It was a quiet achievement—the limited edition of 250 copies did not rock the literary world—but it gave her personal satisfaction. Possibly few literary critics even noticed the slim volume of twenty-six poems. But she had not written them for public applause. She had written them because she had had something she wanted to say. She herself was content.

The flurry of publication did not detain her long from more serious business. There was so little time and so much still to do. "I haven't time," she declared, when pressed to take part in some event away from the studio. "I'm senile you know. My days are numbered and I have a lot of work to do."

For both Girls, an intolerable part of growing old was the erosion of their ability to function on their own. They hung tenaciously to their independence as long as they could. At eighty years of age Florence was still shovelling snow. "I've got a lot of muscle," she claimed proudly. Inevitably, things began to slip. An acquaintance, trying to make light conversation, asked how they managed to look after such a big house. "Well, our friends don't think that we *do* manage," admitted Frances ruefully.

Florence continued to sculpt regularly. Small carvings, especially in sumach, because of its lovely purple grain. And she recast old plasters that had become dog-eared. She was not well but she had the self-discipline to pace herself. Old age was not frightening to Florence as long as she could work.

For Frances it was a different story. Her eyesight was failing. Her lessened mobility began to overtake her. It became almost a major engineering feat to get herself dressed, out of the Church and into a waiting car, in order to attend the meetings that meant so much to her. The time came when she was no longer part of the functioning machinery of art politics. Her impotent body could not rise to her will and she resented it bitterly.

She was saved, briefly, when an interesting small commission came her way. In 1962 Mrs. Herbert Bruce asked Frances to sculpt her husband's hands. Dr. Bruce was a distinguished Toronto surgeon, then ninety-two years of age, and it seemed fitting that his portrait should be a study of his hands.

Frances found the whole conception an intriguing challenge. To portray a surgeon through his hands! She began the project with ardour. But because of those poor old eyes and those arthritic finger joints, the modelling of the hands took longer than anticipated, involving sitting after sitting through an extremely hot summer. As the weeks dragged past, it became difficult for the elderly Dr. Bruce to hold his hands in position in the wilting heat. With the situation bordering on the impossible on both sides, Frances fell back on the diverting powers of her personality. She valiantly entertained her subject with fascinating tales of her youth and various experiences, and a strong empathy developed between the artist and the doctor.

The sculpted hands, meanwhile, made only painful progress.

Frances' conception of them was splendid. Dr. Bruce had short but powerful and sensitive hands. Frances had placed one resting on its side, curved slightly, as if representing a place of refuge. The other, the right hand, was also on its side but raised slightly at the wrist, the index finger lifted in a position of sensitive probing. It was the raised finger that was agonizingly difficult to achieve. In the heat the clay became very soft and the finger kept drooping, which upset the balance of the whole composition. Frances simply could not see to work with the necessary agility. And yet her sense of artistic integrity would not allow her to leave the work until she had been at least modestly successful. Finally, the work was finished and cast (including, inadvertently, her best metal rasp in the base of the plaster). Frances was satisfied. She had captured the essence of Bruce's work as a surgeon; she had interpreted his hands. It was her final work.

Close on the heels of this near-disaster came an event that proved a source of warm satisfaction to both the Girls. As Frances and Florence approached the fifty-year mark of their life together in Toronto, an invitation came from Clare Bice, curator of the Art Museum in London, Ontario. In celebration of those long years of major contribution to the Canadian art scene, would the Girls consider a retrospective exhibition of their work in the London gallery? They would, with the greatest pleasure.

The exhibition was a resounding success. By the time it was mounted in London it included almost all of the Girls' available major works. The two of them had borrowed once again on their deep reserves of strength and stamina to see them through the tremendous job of scrubbing up and mending all the sculptures for this timely airing. The gallery gave every cooperation. Opening night found each carving, bronze and plaster carefully placed, with the lighting just so, the background appropriate, and the various shapes arranged to complement the whole mass. Frances' "Goal Keeper," "The Miner," "Dr. Banting" and "Girl with Fish." Florence's "Justice," "Negress," "A. Y. Jackson," "Varley" and "Chicago." There were nearly seventy pieces in all. Their work had never been shown to such advantage.

It was the last opportunity for open-nighters to experience a preview in company with the Girls. As so often before, they were unconsciously a major attraction in themselves. Frances was resplendent in black velvet, her bulk regally draped in a scarlet Chinese silk stole. Florence was turned out in the frayed dignity of her old grey suit. It was her first appearance at an opening in several years.

The poignancy of this particular occasion threatened to make it a formal "event." But Frances knew exactly how to break the ice. "Hullo, Charlie!" she shouted across the crowd when she spotted their old friend Dr. Charles Comfort. As the head of the National Gallery, he had been invited to open the exhibition.

Throughout its run that November of 1962, there was a large attendance to see the Loring-Wyle sculpture. It aroused more enthusiasm among the gallery-going public than any show within the previous ten years.

There was even a sale. One small plaster reproduction by Florence, for thirty-five dollars.

More than anything, the exhibit gave a tremendous lift to the Girls' morale. Florence felt inspired to tackle one more block of marble. Some years before she had evolved a design in plaster in which she had used the form of a woman to evoke the feeling of a sea wave falling on the shore. She was searching for a way to express the thought, "The tide comes in and the tide goes out but the sea and the shore remain."

As always, she sent the plaster model off to the carver to be roughed out—this time in sparkling Carrara marble. For the first time in all his years of dealing with her, Temporale found Florence difficult to work with. She would not be satisfied. When the stone was returned to the studio for her to finish off the surface, she was even harder on herself. She was eighty-three years old, and she was desperate to condense the whole lifetime of her commitment into this work.

Florence had moved her carving stand into the main studio to take advantage of the lighting from the big skylight and to keep an eye on Frances who was largely confined to the couch where she sat and worked on her papers. The music of the chisel on stone sounded through the building endlessly.

"Oh Florence! Do leave it alone! You're completely ruining it—you're polishing it too much," Frances would remonstrate from across the room.

"Well," Florence would hesitate as she stood back and looked from all angles at the arc of the figure. "Just a slight bit more here that has to be. . . ." Although the figure, with its surging flow, was a fine example of inspired craftsmanship, it never did quite please her. The possibility of perfection lured her on and on.

When a half-hour film of the Girls was made by Christopher Chapman, early in 1965, Florence was featured in one sequence still putting the finishing touches to her "Sea and Shore." She only left off ultimately because she had decided to enter it in the upcoming Ontario Society of Artists exhibition. It was some years since she had been able to offer a new major sculpture for their show, and as a longstanding member of the society, she was happy to be in a position to contribute once again. The carving was transported, with great difficulty, down to the Art Gallery of Toronto where the jurors were to meet to choose the show. In due course a letter arrived at the studio for Florence, from the Ontario Society of Artists. She was expecting it. Opening it as a matter of course she removed the enclosed slip of paper. Then she froze.

"Sea and Shore" had not been accepted for exhibition.

If she had been younger she would have recovered from the blow. But at eighty-four the resiliency was gone. "Why?" she asked, bewildered. It was certainly not because she had polished it too much. Perhaps the self-assertion of the new, more vigorous art expression allowed no place for the old.

The episode infuriated Frances, all the more so because she was powerless to do anything about it. Her pathetic frustration was like that of a great wounded lion no longer able to stand up and do battle. It was getting late for both the Girls.

The final year together in the Church was agonizing. Frances' physical condition began to slip downhill disastrously. She could barely walk; she could barely see. There were frightening periods of delusions. An enforced stay in the hospital proved unbearable to her. Calling up her old fire, she managed, against all entreaty, to get herself back home. Florence, who had almost completely slipped into senility during Frances' stay in the hospital, recovered remarkably, and steeled herself to give all her remaining strength to support her ailing partner.

There was still the odd spark of the old levity between them. The matter of the canes was always good for a chuckle. Frances was in the habit of throwing these two indispensable supports down the stairwell, ahead of her, when descending for supper. They would dance and clatter from step to step before crashing out into the dining room from the doorway of the walled-in staircase. With a good-natured laugh she would retrieve them at the bottom, and proceed to the table. It was a traumatic experience for unprepared dinner guests.

"When I depart from this world, and want to come back and communicate with you," she told Florence and their dear friend Jean Irving, "listen for the canes. When you hear them you'll know it's me with a message for you."

The time came when she could no longer make it downstairs, when each step was taken by sheer force of will. Florence would put her wiry sculptor's arm around the helpless bulk and literally haul Frances out of the confining bedroom to the couch in the studio. "Are you comfortable, Queenie?" she would ask when Frances had been ensconced in a throne of supporting pillows. It was stark daily drama in which not even the closest friend would dare to participate. The acting out of the endurance of the one partner and the compassion of the other.

Then came Keith's death—a bitter blow for both of them, but softened, mercifully, by their ebbing touch with reality.

The bleakness of those days was brightened for Florence by the appearance of a neighbour's pregnant cat. As her time drew near, she rejected a devoted family back home and attached herself more and more closely to Florence. Frances thought the expectant mother should be returned home, and she was indeed, regularly sent along in that direction, only to reappear at the Church. Then one morning Agnes was met at the door by a radiant Florence. "Sh-sh-sh!" she whispered conspiratorially. "Don't tell Frances!" Leading the way to a crevice formed between adjoining work benches, she revealed the proud cat with several newborn kittens—all comfortably settled in a softly-lined box, obviously provided expressly for the birth. Florence had done it again.

The Girls were old; they were ailing hopelessly; and they were passé. But they were to make a final farewell appearance.

The Chapman film, screened on television late in the spring of 1965, sympathetically thrust the two sculptors once again into public consciousness. Accolades poured into the Church from all sources. The tributes touched the Girls deeply, yet when a commercial gallery approached them for a two-man show in the autumn, they responded with surprisingly little interest. They were too tired.

"Where have most of your sculptures come to rest?" they had been asked only a short time before.

"Right here!" they had answered. And at this late stage they were quite content to have their work around them.

Still, they were living far below what had become popularly known as the poverty level, and it was pointed out to them that a show at this juncture of time and interest would have every chance of being a financial success. At the urging of some of their friends, they acquiesced, rather disinterestedly, to an exhibition at the Pollock Gallery early in the new year.

The great day arrived. Dignified preparations had been made for a triumphant opening to be attended briefly by the Girls themselves, Frances in a wheelchair. Alas, never one to fall in quietly with best-laid plans, Frances collapsed before leaving home for the exhibition, and was rushed immediately to the hospital. Within the week, Florence also fell ill, and was taken to a hospital. They ended their days in a nursing home in Newmarket, where, separated after nearly sixty years together, they seldom inquired for one another. Life had apparently ceased for them when they left each other and the Church.

Their exhibition had a marked success. There were substantial sales to various institutions and collections that had not earlier considered their work. In the grand tradition of artists down through the ages, the Girls had left the scene before their audience had come to a full appreciation of their achievement.

EPILOGUE

Florence Wyle died on January 14, 1968. Even in the last stages of senility, she was a human being of uncommon inner beauty.

Frances Loring died three weeks later, on February 5, 1968. To the last, even in her delusions, she was a fascinating and compelling personality.

Two very remarkable, vivid people passed from the stage. Their lives had touched and given spark to an incredible assortment of people. The terms of their will (which banked shrewdly on posthumous interest in their work) ensured that their active concern for sculptors would continue long after they were gone. Their own sculpture was to be sold, and the proceeds used to form a fund to purchase works by young, unknown sculptors, to be presented to various public galleries across the country. The Church was left to the Royal Canadian Academy, to be used or disposed of at its discretion for the stimulation of Canadian art in all its aspects, and "for the particular development and encouragement of, and education in, Canadian sculpture."

The Girls had stood as beacons in the development of Canadian sculpture. Their own work reflected the school of art in which they were moulded, but their inspiration and direction came from life itself. The Girls' work in all instances was honest. They had absolute integrity within their conception. It was this integrity of spirit, coupled with a selfless devotion to the cause of artists, that lifted their influence to a plane beyond that represented by their work alone.

Their years of struggle must be seen through their eyes to be understood.

"Is sculpture worth it?" they were asked toward the end of their lives.

Florence answered for both of them, with uncompromising truth. "Depends on what you want from life. If you want to make lots of money—well, few are permanently famous. But if you want to create beauty in lasting form, then sculpture is worthwhile. Most of the rewards are apt to be spiritual."

For the Girls, sculpture had been magnificently worthwhile.

INDEX OF PEOPLE MENTIONED

Laliberté, Alfred, 24, 43, 45
Lawson, Larry, 11
Long, Marion, 62

Massey, Vincent, 97
Meroz, Jean, 100
Mulligan, Charles, 18
Murphy, John, 58, 79
MacIver, Edith, 38
MacIver, Keith, 10, 37, 38, 40,
    57, 61, 93, 113
McCarthy, Pearl, 100, 106, 108
McCurry, H. O., 54, 65, 72, 87,
    102
McGibbon, Pauline, 95, 96
McLaughlin, R. S., 54

Newton, Lilias, 62

Ogilvie, Will, 39, 41
Ongley, David, 95, 96

Parsons, Vera, 99
Pearson, John, 26, 54

Radley, Mr. & Mrs. Bernard, 82
Redsell, Pauline, 73, 103

Savage, Anne, 41
Schreiber, Charlotte, 62
Sommerville, William, 62, 63, 67
Stewart, Donald, 73, 74
Suzor-Coté, Marc Aurèle, 24
Swanson, Pete, 40

Taft, Laredo, 17, 18, 20
Temporale, Louis, 66, 104, 111
Tracy, Arthur, 74
Trenka, Stephen, 74

Varley, F. H., 27

Walker, Sir Edmund, 29
Williams, Edith, 84, 85, 88
Williams, Gwendolyn, 11, 40
Wyn Wood, Elizabeth, 43, 45,
    72, 74